RECA

Navigating the winding road to success

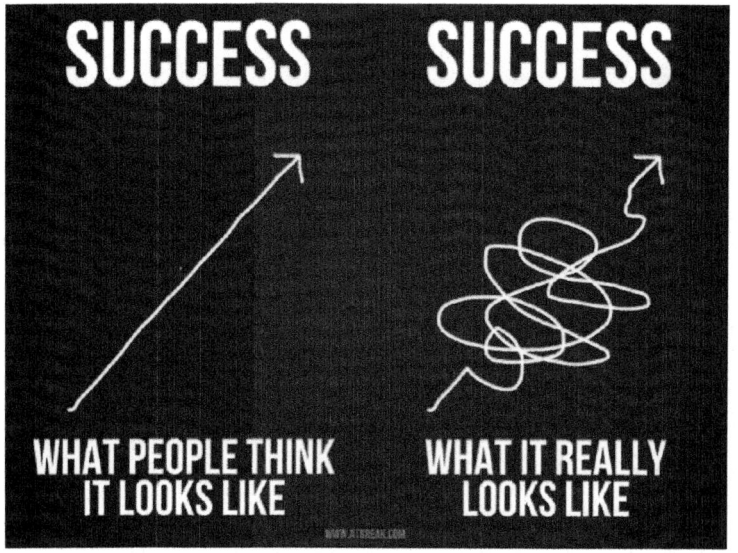

JEREMY BLOOM

© 2023 Jeremy Bloom

All rights reserved. No part of this book may be reproduced or transmitted in any form or by any means, electronic or mechanical, including photocopying, recording, or by any information storage and retrieval system, without permission in writing from the publisher.

JRB Property LLC
7931 s Broadway
#103
Littleton, Co 80122

ISBN: 9798386930127

Printed in the United States of America

Cover design by Kiley Del Valle
Interior design by Natalia Junqueira
Editing by Steve Johnson

First Edition: April 2023

Nic —

Hope you enjoy the book, we appreciate the partnership

PRAISE FOR RECALIBRATE

"Jeremy is one of the most compelling entrepreneurs I've ever worked with—actually, one of the most compelling individuals I've ever worked with. Always striving for the next goal, taking each setback as an opportunity to learn, surrounding himself with people he can learn from. Jeremy's never-give-up attitude is infectious and makes him extremely effective."

Seth Levine

"Jeremy's super smart and he gets the big picture. He realized that after sports he would need to do something more. He surrounded himself with very strong, very bright individuals who shared their insights, advice, and best practices. Now you too can learn those attributes in this book."

Apolo Ohno

"Throughout my life, I have come across incredible leaders, but Jeremy's ability to accomplish so many different feats consistently astounds me. As a friend and board member of Integrate, I am continually impressed by the way that he adapts and succeeds in any situation, even when it seems unachievable. This book helps to unlock your full potential by providing a roadmap on how to use adversity to strengthen your chances of ultimate success."

Reggie Bradford

"Part of what has made Jeremy's life so remarkable is that he takes on challenges and doesn't look back. When something doesn't work out, he learns why and uses that knowledge to better himself.

His book is the proverbial kick in the ass that most of us need when we start retreating or giving up on a challenge or a goal."

Brad Feld

"Jeremy is proof that mindset is everything. He brings together the best people and supercharges them with his unique energy and inspiration. His Olympian work ethic and discipline works in the boardroom as well as it did on the ski slopes and football field. He will inspire you, too."

Bing Gordon

CONTENTS

Acknowledgments 1

CHAPTER ONE: Recalibrating 5

CHAPTER TWO: Football & Skiing 11

CHAPTER THREE: 48-hour rule 25

CHAPTER FOUR: Give Up Your Need To Win? 33

CHAPTER FIVE: The Roadmap For Recalibration 41

CHAPTER SIX: Recalibrating A New Path 53

CHAPTER SEVEN: Leadership, Chemistry, And Victims 67

CHAPTER EIGHT: Building A Locked-Arms Culture 83

CHAPTER NINE: The Roller Coaster Ride 101

CHAPTER TEN: A Rising tide lifts all boats 113

EPILOGUE: The trail to purpose 131

Incredible Stories of Recalibration 135

One: The Unstoppable Drive - The Story of Wilma Rudolph 137

Two: The Power of Transformation - The Story of Bethany Hamilton 141

Three: Scaling New Heights - The Remarkable Story of Erik Weihenmayer 145

Four: From Civil Rights Activist to Congresswoman: The Inspiring Journey of Barbara Lee 149

FIVE: Scaling the Heights - The Story of Arunima Sinha 155

SIX: Rising from the Ashes - The Resilient Journey of Turia Pitt 157

SEVEN: Overcoming Failure - The Journey of Frida Kahlo to Artistic Greatness 161

EIGHT: Defying Gravity - The Courageous Story of Jessica Cox 165

NINE: An Unbreakable Will - The Remarkable Story of Dr. Sakena Yacoobi 169

TEN: Rising from the Shadows - The Magical Journey of J.K. Rowling 173

ELEVEN: Turning the Tide - The Inspiring Story of João Carlos Martins 177

TWELVE: Rising Above - The Story of Stephen Hawking 181

THIRTEEN: From Tragedy to Triumph - The Story of Malala Yousafzai 185

FOURTEEN: The Unbreakable Spirit - The Story of Nelson Mandela 189

FIFTEEN: Soaring to New Heights - The Story of Nkosi Johnson 193

SIXTEEN: The Unwavering Resilience - The Story of Chris Gardner ... 197

SEVENTEEN: Temple Grandin - Overcoming Challenges to Become an Expert in Animal Behavior 201

EIGHTEEN: The Unbreakable Spirit - The Story of Nick Vujicic 205

NINETEEN: The Long Road to Fame - The Story of Viola Davis 209

TWENTY: A Sky Full of Dreams - The Story of Chris Martin 215

About the AUTHOR 219

ACKNOWLEDGMENTS

My parents, Char and Larry, have always been my rock. They've stood by me through thick and thin, and their belief in me has never wavered. When I was a boy, they encouraged me to dream big and chase my passions, no matter how daunting they seemed. And as I grew into a man, they continued to support me every step of the way, guiding me with their wisdom and unwavering love.

My siblings, Jordan and Molly, are two of the finest people I've ever known. They've always been my role models, inspiring me to aim high and strive for excellence in everything I do. Their influence has helped shape me into the man I am today, and I will always be grateful for their love and guidance.

And then there are my grandparents, Donna and Jerry. Their love and support have been a constant throughout my life, and their wisdom has helped guide me through some of the toughest challenges I've faced. Whether it was a word of encouragement or a gentle nudge in the right direction, they always knew exactly what I needed to hear. I will always be grateful for their presence in my life, and I will always cherish the memories we've shared together.

Last but certainly not least, I am filled with gratitude for my beloved wife, Mariah, and our precious children, Violet and Hendrix. They are the light of my life, and their unwavering love and support have been a constant source of strength and inspiration. Mariah's unwavering love has been my rock through all of life's ups and downs, and I am forever grateful for her unwavering devotion.

Our children, Violet and Hendrix, are the greatest gifts life has ever bestowed upon us. Their laughter, their boundless energy, and their pure, unadulterated love bring meaning and purpose to every single day. I am honored to be their father, and I cherish the time we spend together as a family.

To Mariah, Violet, and Hendrix, I say this: thank you. Thank you for being my partners on this incredible journey called life. Thank you for filling my days with joy, laughter, and love. And thank you for helping me become the man I am today.

CHAPTER ONE
RECALIBRATING

Have you ever experienced a time in your life when things didn't go as planned? How would you rate your ability to handle adversity? Do you wish you could have moved on faster and turned a difficult moment into a positive experience?

I believe that the most essential skill for achieving success and leading a happy life is the ability to quickly bounce back after setbacks. Unfortunately, many people go through life unprepared to deal with the ups and downs that come their way. There is no class in elementary, middle, or even high school that teaches this crucial topic.

Throughout my athletic career, I heard coaches, teammates, and family members say that setbacks make us stronger, and adversity makes us more resilient. However, this wasn't always the case for me. In the early stages of my career, each defeat would cause me to lose confidence and doubt my future in the two sports that I loved. It wasn't until I became a diligent student of resilience that I was able to unlock my full potential and become one of the best freestyle skiers in the world.

If you struggle to bounce back from setbacks and move on quickly, the good news is that this is not a skill that you are either born with or without. It is a learned technique, much like a muscle, that gets stronger with practice. In this book, I will share insights and anecdotes that I have learned from my own experiences and observations of some of the most accomplished people in the world.

I want to start by assuring you that this book is crafted with the intention of making every page count. As an avid reader myself, I understand the value of time and how frustrating it can be to read books that seem to drag on with unnecessary details. Therefore, I've made it my mission to eliminate any redundant information and present only the most impactful insights. Without further ado, let's dive right in.

We are all uniquely human, despite our differences. We were all born to mothers, we all need oxygen to survive, and we will all fall short of our own expectations numerous times throughout our lives. Some of us allow these failures to shatter our confidence, while others learn to use these powerful moments to recalibrate their roadmap to success.

Failing to meet our goals and expectations doesn't feel good and can be embarrassing, demotivating, and cause us to doubt our abilities. However, it doesn't have to be this way. In fact, I would argue that this isn't even what life intends for us during these times.

To understand the evolutionary purpose of adversity, we need only to look at our infancy. In the early years of our lives, failure was our greatest teacher. We fell thousands of times before learning how to walk properly. We mixed up the sounds of every word in the dictionary before learning to speak correctly. And, as the father of a one-year-old daughter, I can tell you firsthand that potty training is no walk in the park. But in this formative stage of life, we simply use our failures as a data point – a road sign showing us the way to our destination. We didn't care who saw us fall, we didn't question our ability or chances of success; we just got up, recalibrated, and continued our journey.

So, why do we often avoid these valuable data points of adversity as adults? The answer is likely obvious, but the psychology behind it may not be. The main physiological difference between infants and adults is that infants aren't born with an ego – that little voice in our head that constantly analyzes the world around us, trying to define our self-esteem and self-importance.

The ego can be a force for good, but more often it's where success and dreams go to die. When we try new things as adults, our ego often tells us that we are not good enough and we shouldn't embarrass ourselves by trying. This fear of failure and embarrassment becomes a powerful obstacle that keeps us from pursuing our goals and dreams.

But, as I mentioned earlier, resilience is a learned technique that we can all develop with practice. To bounce back from setbacks and move on quickly, we need to learn how to quiet our ego and focus on the task at hand. We must learn to embrace our failures and use them as opportunities to learn and grow. And, most importantly, we must develop a growth mindset – the belief that we can always improve and become better versions of ourselves.

In the following chapters, I will delve deeper into these concepts and provide practical strategies for developing resilience and a growth mindset. I will also share stories and examples from my own life and the lives of others who have excelled in their respective fields.

Following the epilogue , you will be introduced to twenty awe-inspiring stories of individuals who have faced incredible adversity and used it to their advantage, recalibrating their lives to achieve greatness. These extraordinary people teach us the importance of perseverance, resilience, and the power of the human spirit.

You will read about Arunima Sinha, a former national-level volleyball player from India, who overcame the loss of her leg in a horrific accident to become the first female amputee to scale Mount Everest. Her unyielding determination in the face of adversity serves as a shining example of what can be achieved with unwavering resolve.

Next, immerse yourself in the life of Bethany Hamilton, a professional surfer who made a remarkable comeback after losing her left arm in a shark attack. Through courage, faith, and an unwavering passion for her sport, she defied the odds and continues to inspire others with her incredible story.

Then, delve into the story of João Carlos Martins, a Brazilian pianist and conductor who refused to let multiple setbacks, including neurological conditions and physical injuries, prevent him from pursuing his passion for music. Through constant recalibration and adaptation, Martins has continued to inspire others with his exceptional talent and dedication to helping underprivileged musicians.

These powerful narratives offer a glimpse into the lives of individuals who have overcome seemingly insurmountable obstacles to achieve greatness. As you read their stories, you will undoubtedly be inspired by their courage, tenacity, and the transformative power of recalibration in the face of adversity.

I hope that this book will serve as a guide and inspiration for you on your own journey to becoming exceptional at anything and enjoying a meaningful life.

CHAPTER TWO
FOOTBALL & SKIING

When I was ten years old, I told my parents that I wanted to ski in the Olympics and be drafted into the NFL.

Both of my parents, who have a healthy disrespect for the impossible, told me that I could accomplish both of those goals if I attacked my dreams with everything I had. I learned in that moment that it wasn't enough to just dream about something; if I wanted to accomplish it I would need to follow their advice and attack.

The promise that I showed in both sports varied widely as a young kid. In skiing, from a very young age people viewed me as a kid prodigy. I grew up skiing at Keystone Mountain in Colorado and people hooted and hollered from the chairlift as I ripped down a mogul run and threw a heli.

My ski coaches often told my parents that I had a special ability and a real chance to make the US Ski Team someday if I focused all my attention on the sport.

In football, pretty much the opposite is true. I was the smallest kid on every football field I ever stepped onto, and the narrative was consistent: "You're going to get hurt playing football. Skiing is your future, not football."

But I did have two things that nobody could match, and one was speed. I was fast, and I mean *really* fast. Nobody could catch me if I hit the open field. The other was heart. I wouldn't allow anyone to outwork me and prided myself at being the first one to practice and the last one to leave, every single day. By age eleven, my dad reached his limit of coaching abilities and signed me up for the freestyle ski team at Breckenridge, Colorado. Two of the greatest mogul coaches in history happened to coach there: Scott Rawles—who later became my Olympic team coach for many years—and John Dowling, who went on to lead Canada's Olympic Team.

Not long after becoming part of Team Breckenridge, I also started playing Pop Warner football, where my dad was my head coach.

Then, at 15, I became the youngest male skier in history to make the U.S. Mogul Freestyle Ski Team. My ski coaches and the federation insisted that I quit playing football and move to a ski academy in the mountains. They said as a part-time skier who was also dedicated to another sport, I had very little chance of becoming successful and that it wasn't fair to my fellow teammates if I missed team camps for another sport. This was one of the first big moments in my life that I learned of the importance of recalibrating.

I was in a pickle, and I only had two options. I either obey the national team coaches and give up on my dream to play football or I figure out a way to change their minds. I elected for the latter, created a written petition, and handed it out to all my teammates. The petition asked one simple question. "Do you think it's unfair to you if Jeremy misses a team camp due to his position on the Loveland High School Football Team?" Everyone of my teammates checked the box "no" and the national team coaches had no other choice than to begrudgingly allow me to play both sports.

In my freshman year of high school, I played quarterback and defensive back. My sophomore year, at the urging of my coach, Tony Davis, a former star running back at Nebraska, I switched to wide receiver and this move allowed me to start on the varsity team. Midway through my senior year of high school, the University of Colorado offered me a full scholarship to play football.

Meanwhile, at 17, I was now competing and winning freestyle events on the Nor-Am tour, the tour just below World Cup. That same year, I also won the Papa John's Bumps n Jumps pro tour, scoring a brand new Chevy Trailblazer along the way.

Winning the Nor-Am tour and Bumps n Jumps in the same season cemented me as the number one skier not already competing on the World Cup Tour.

After the season ended, it seemed obvious that I would be chosen to compete in a full World Cup season the following year given my domination in the amateur ranks. But I was not selected. I was confused, frustrated, and very unhappy. Without World Cup starts it was nearly impossible for me to make the Olympic team the next year. Here was another important moment of recalibration for me as a young up-and-coming skier. I decided I was going to use this disappointment to fuel my desire to work even harder than I did before and dominate the sport to a degree that coaches could never take another opportunity away from me.

I took that newfound anger, aggression, and determination to a pre-Olympic fall camp in El Colorado, Chile where I showed up in the best shape of my life.

For the 22-day camp I was the first one on the ski hill and the last one off. I was skiing top-to-bottom runs like my life depended on it. After each day, I literally limped back to my apartment, soaked in an ice bath for 20 minutes, and try to get myself ready for the next day. I was as hungry as ever to prove to my coaches that they made a terrible decision.

I had to leave camp four days early to fly back for fall football camp in Colorado. The day before I was set to leave, U.S. Ski Team coaches Donnie St. Pierre, Liz McIntyre, and Scott Rawles asked to meet with me.

We met in the hotel lobby, and they told me they had never seen anyone attack a training camp like I just had and wanted to offer me one World Cup start in Tignes, France. If I finished in the top 12 in Tignes, I would be able to compete the rest of the way and have a chance to make the Olympic Team.

When I landed in Colorado, I called my mom and dad and then met with my football coach, Gary Barnett. I told Coach Barnett that I committed to play football that year and if he didn't want me to try to make the Olympic Ski Team, I wouldn't do it.

Coach looked at me and told me something I will never forget. "Jeremy, I'm going to treat you like my son right now. I want you to go for your dream of becoming an Olympian and your full scholarship will be waiting for you here at CU next year. We will be cheering for you. Go make it happen."

With the blessing from my football coach, the next stop was Park City, Utah, to train full time with Chris Marchetti. He was introduced to me by my agent, Andy Carroll, and training with him turned out to be one of the best decisions of my skiing career. We took our training to the next level. Sometimes I would wake up at 3 A.M. and hike a mountain because I knew my competitors were sleeping. It was intense but I loved every second of it.

As the season approached, I felt butterflies about having one shot to make the Olympic team. I flew to Tignes for my first World Cup on the same day that the University of Colorado beat Texas to win the Big 12 title. I knew the pressure was on; not only did I turn away a chance to be part of a championship winning football team but my dream of becoming an Olympian would be decided at this one competition.

In my qualification run, a big gust of wind covered the course with snow while I was skiing. The judges lost sight of me for a split second, so they made me take another run. That was a lucky break because I had made a small mistake on that first run that would have cost me a shot in the finals. In my next qualification run I told myself to let it loose. Don't hold back anything. My second run was much better, and I qualified—in 12th place!

I couldn't believe it. All I needed was a top-12 finish to be able to ski the rest of the World Cups and I qualified in 12th by ten one-hundredths of a point. You couldn't wipe the smile off my face if you tried. In the finals, I really nailed it, skiing one of the best competitive runs ever and landing on the podium in third place, qualifying for the 2002 Olympic Team.

While I didn't get the finish I was hoping for at those games, I ended the season as the world's number-one ranked skier and won my first World Cup Overall trophy. Over the next four years I would go on to win three world championships, 11 world cup gold medals, 26 podiums and became the youngest skier ever to be inducted into the United States Skiing Hall of Fame.

Back on Campus: A Football Dream Builds

I arrived back on campus for my freshman football season in the glow of a national spotlight, but it made me feel uncomfortable. I didn't want the attention on me; I just wanted to focus on making the team. To make things worse, the NCAA told me they were not going to allow me to play college football and still get paid by my skiing sponsors. I decided to fight the NCAA in court over this decision, which didn't exactly help remove the spotlight. The case captured national attention and the interest of sports fans all over the world. Here was a nineteen-year-old kid who represented his country in one sport and The University of Colorado in another and the NCAA was trying to take away everything that he worked so hard for. For reasons that I could write another book about, the district court in Boulder ruled in favor of the NCAA and I was forced to forgo about $500,000 of skiing-related endorsements that funded my career.

Many people at the time thought it a foolish decision to give up all those endorsements for the chance to play football. After all, I was a five-foot-nine, 175-pound receiver trying to play for a team that just won the Big 12 championship. Most people thought that I would never see the playing field.

But I was confident in my ability and knew I was the fastest guy on the field. At the season opener against our in-state rivals Colorado State, I was not in the starting lineup as a receiver and was listed third on the punt return team. It was a tight game for three quarters and we were down 10–0 heading into the fourth.

During a TV commercial break, I heard Coach Barnett call my name. I ran up to him and said, "Ya coach, what's up?"

"Jeremy, I want you to go return this punt."

Without thinking, I said, "No problem," and grabbed my helmet. As I jogged onto the field, the same field where the Denver Broncos played, the moment really hit me. I looked around and saw 80,000 people, national TV cameras, friends, and family in the stadium . . . and here I was about to return the first punt of my life for the college I always dreamt of playing for.

All I remember thinking was, "Just don't drop the ball."

The punt seemed to hang in the air forever but as it came down, it did so right into my chest.

I caught the ball, took two steps up the middle, then cut to the right sideline. I saw my teammates in front of me set up a great looking wall and I raced down the sidelines.

I made a few defenders miss and before I knew it, my hands were in the air, and I was in the end zone celebrating. The first time I touched the ball for the CU Buffs, I took a punt back 75 yards to the house and scored my first collegiate touchdown. I remember looking around seeing my teammates going crazy and fans jumping up and down and I thought to myself, "This is why I turned down that money." No amount of money could compare to that feeling and that experience.

For two years at college, I had the time of my life. I returned punts and played wide receiver for the Colorado Buffaloes. I set several school records, including the longest pass reception in history at 96 yards, and after my freshman season I was named First Team All-American.

But I had a problem. I still loved to ski and there was another Olympics forthcoming. Yet, at this point I was broke and no longer had the funds to pay for skiing's significant expense. It was 2004 and without sponsorship support I would not be able to train for the 2006 Games.

So, I publicly drew a line in the sand and told the NCAA I was going to accept skiing-related endorsements so I could train and compete for the United States in the next Olympics. And that I was not leaving school if they didn't want me there, they would have to kick me out.

They waited seven months to do so and in August 2004, right before fall football camp opened, they declared me permanently ineligible, and I lost out on my opportunity to be the number one receiver on my Junior and Senior teams.

I was heartbroken. I couldn't believe an organization, at which I had never met a single person, could take away something I worked so hard for. But the decision was made. I needed to recalibrate quickly, so I packed my bags, left college, and began training for the Torino Olympics.

Torino

As the 2006 Torino Games kicked off, I was ready and prepared. Standing in the starting gate, I thought about all the years of training and sacrifice. I thought about my mom down below in the grandstand and my dad back home in Colorado watching the live broadcast on Channel 9 news. I thought about all my friends and family around the world watching me on TV. I flashed back to the years I spent competing in regional competitions around Colorado, the phone call I received at age 15 when I found out that I had made the U.S. National Team, and the thousands of hours spent preparing myself for this moment. Images shot through my mind of the journey that had brought me to this point. I remembered the time, at 10 years old, when I first watched Olympics mogul skiing with my dad and mom.

My dad has a passion for the Olympics that goes back to the Carl Lewis days at the 1984 Games and continues to this day. When a U.S. athlete stands atop the podium and "The Star-Spangled Banner" plays, it is a powerfully emotional moment. My dad was my first football coach and ski coach, and my hero. I wanted nothing more in my life than to win an Olympic gold medal, not only for myself but also for my family. The thought of my family watching me as I stood on top of that Olympic podium, with a gold medal wrapped around my neck, was a major driving force in my lifelong quest.

One Move, One Moment

As I slid into the starting gate, I got my first glimpse of the 230-meter mogul course. It was a beautiful night in Torino; the snow sparkled off the bright lights like a Manhattan sidewalk on a warm summer evening.

I went over my three keys:

1. *Mind like a river.* It's normal to have self-defeating thoughts but they only mess you up if they stick in your mind. I pictured a fast-moving river from the front of my head to the back and any thoughts that came up were quickly swept away. This was one of the best and most powerful mental tools that I ever learned in sports.

2. *Live downstairs.* I imagined myself in a windowless basement that had no connection to the outside world. This helped me drown out the noise, cameras in my face, thousands of people in the grandstand below, the scores of my fellow skiers who already finished their runs, and other distractions. It really helped me stay extremely focused on the task at hand.

3. *Focus on your skills.* I knew that I had worked harder than anyone on that ski hill and in doing so developed all the skills necessary to get me down the mountain in perfect form. Having the ultimate confidence in your skills is a very powerful mindset and reduces the anxiety of sports, especially on a world stage.

I had an unusual sense of confidence that day. I wasn't nervous and I knew exactly what I needed to do.

"Three, two, one," over the loudspeaker and I pushed out of the gate. I felt the snow under my skis and quickly got into the top jump. I nailed my takeoff and landed my 720 iron-cross perfectly. As I landed, I accelerated faster and faster. The snow was a bit icier than it had been in training. My knees broke form for a split second (did the judges see that?) and I felt a there-and-gone moment of self-doubt but fought through it, got it back together quickly, and flew into the bottom air. The takeoff on my D-spin 720 was solid and I blazed through the bottom section of the course to the finish line.

As I crossed the line, I knew I had made one very small mistake but didn't know if it would cost me or not. It felt like time stopped as I awaited my score, with a knotted gut and spaghetti-tangled nerves wondering how the judges would react to the one-inch mistake I made on the hill.

My score came up. I was in fourth place with two skiers to go. I couldn't believe it. One inch was the difference between standing on the podium that day and getting knocked out of medal contention.

I held it together as I made my way through the media gauntlet. I tried to smile and say the right things, but it was tough to mask my disappointment. After talking to the media, my mom came over, hugged me, and told me she was very proud of me. And I remember saying, "What the fuck are you proud of; I just lost the Olympics."

My mom was my biggest supporter. She flew all over the world to see me compete and had not missed a single football game I played in during high school and college. However, she always cared much more about how I treated others and how I handled winning and losing than she cared about which place I got.

When I returned to my apartment in Torino, I closed the door, sat down on the bed, and lost it in a torrent of emotions and tears. I wanted to crawl outside of my body because the pain felt unbearable. It was the lowest moment of my athletic life; I felt defeated.

Steve Jobs once famously said that you can only connect the dots of life looking in reverse. What I didn't know that day that I do now is this was one of the most important days of my life in the classroom of how to master recalibration. It was this day, in this moment of despair, that I came up with the idea to give myself 48 hours. Forty-eight hours to do whatever it took to learn from this experience. To dissect every second of it and boil it all down to actionable lessons. I mentally committed to myself that after that 48-hour window I was going to move 100 mph to whatever was next. Ever since, the 48-hour rule has been a game changer for me in my personal, athletic, and professional life. I'll dig deeper into the concept in the next chapter.

The next day, I boarded a plane to Indianapolis for the 2006 NFL Combine, the showcase for college football players to perform physical and mental tests in front of scouts, coaches, and general managers. It was the prelude to being drafted by a pro team.

I was excited to use the learnings and energy from Torino to recalibrate my roadmap for success in the NFL.

I performed well at the combine, running the 40-yard dash in 4.4 seconds, which wasn't my fastest time but given I had just taken off the ski boots the scouts were very impressed.

Two months after competing in Torino, on April 30, 2006, I was selected by the Philadelphia Eagles in the fifth round of the NFL draft.

I had gone from my second Olympics to making an NFL roster in a few short months. I was living out my childhood dreams on the world's biggest stages.

I spent two seasons with the Eagles and a season with the Pittsburgh Steelers. I had a wonderful time playing in the NFL, sharing the locker room with guys like Donavan McNabb, Brian Dawkins, Ben Roethlisberger, Hines Ward, and Troy Polamalu. And it was incredible to be coached by legendary coaches like Mike Tomlin and Andy Reid. But the NFL ended up having a bigger impact on my life off the football field than on it. I took advantage of an NFL continuing education program that allowed me to take MBA classes at the University of Pennsylvania's Wharton School. It was there where I was first inspired to get into tech and start my own company someday.

I just had to recalibrate, with a 48-hour head start.

CHAPTER THREE
48-HOUR RULE

When it comes to recalibrating, I appreciate how John Maxwell describes it in his book, The Difference Maker: "There are only two types of people in this world when it comes to dealing with discouragement: splatters and bouncers. When splatters reach rock bottom, they fall apart and stay stuck at the bottom. On the other hand, when bouncers reach rock bottom, they pull themselves together and bounce back."

The most resilient bouncers I know have a methodical approach to analyzing the situation with a learner's mindset, eliminating the possibility that the outcome defines them, and quickly implementing the lessons they have learned. While certain personality traits may be more inclined towards being a bouncer or a splatter, this is mainly a learned skill rather than something we are born with.

The Power of Deadlines: One crucial step in recalibrating is not to take experiences personally. Our failed relationship does not define us, nor does the college that rejected us or the company that let us go. These are simply necessary and important steps in our journey of life. Rather than hiding from these moments, embrace them as a baby might, learning from every move with no wasted motion or thought. During times of recalibration, consider the following:

Be selfish. This is your time to grow, so do whatever you need to do to process the information. For me, I prefer to be alone during these times and not be bothered.

Reflect objectively. What went wrong? What could you have done differently? What lessons can you take with you?

Once you reach the deadline, be prescriptive with yourself, move forward at 100 mph and do not look back.

Of course, we are all different, so the amount of time you need to recalibrate may vary. Not every disappointment requires 48 hours, while some may need more time. Remember that the length of time is less important than setting a deadline.

When I won my first World Championship gold medal in skiing, I used three mental points of focus: keep my mind like a river, live downstairs, and focus on my skills. I mentioned these keys briefly in Chapter Two, but I want to expand on them for those who are interested in learning more."

Mind Like a River

The concept of "mind like a river" was something I developed to ensure that no thought would get stuck in my mind before a competition or during my performance. Necessity truly is the mother of invention, and I came up with this mental framework after a mental breakdown I experienced at a World Cup in France. I had qualified in first place, which meant I would be the last person to ski in the finals. One of my bitter rivals was winning the competition, and if I didn't have a great run, he was going to win. I didn't like the idea of this guy winning, and all I could think about was beating him. As I launched off the top jump, I landed flat on my back and completely forgot how to do a trick that I had mastered thousands of times. I allowed a single thought to get in the way of my focus on my skills.

Self-defeating thoughts are normal; we all have them. But the next time you have a self-defeating thought just before a big event, business pitch, company presentation, media interviews, or critical meeting, consider picturing a fast-moving river sweeping all the thoughts out of your brain quickly and efficiently. If this doesn't work the first time, don't give up. It took me hundreds of times trying this out before it really caught on.

Using mental imagery like this can also be very effective when you need to react quickly. We don't always have 48 hours to come to terms with adversity. For example, if a hockey or soccer goalie holds onto negative feelings about the goal they just gave up, they are more likely to give up another one. If I dropped a pass in football and didn't let the bad feeling that came with it flow out of my mind, I knew I would be more likely to drop another one. Why? Because holding on to negative thoughts about the past makes us doubt ourselves. Athletes can't dwell on mistakes and must regain focus quickly. This is also the case in business. Consider a stockbroker making market trades. They simply can't let a drop in the market consume them or they will miss the next opportunities to jump back in and make profitable decisions. Many world-class coaches teach athletes how to have a short memory, and this is a powerful skill.

Living Downstairs

The second skill I attempted to master was a concept called "living downstairs." We all encounter distractions that are beyond our control and many of them involve significant pressure. In my athletic career, these outside distractions included knowing that my parents were traveling halfway around the world to watch me compete, a nationally televised event, Sports Illustrated picking me to win, or a girl I was trying to impress.

In the corporate setting, these distractions can often include fear of letting down colleagues, noise from a big competitor, or a naysayer trying to undermine your confidence. When I really need to focus but face a lot of outside noise, I close my eyes and picture myself walking downstairs into a windowless cellar where no outside thoughts or noise can get in. And if those thoughts ever manage to enter the cellar of my mind, I simply picture a fast-moving river carrying them away immediately.

Focus on Your Skills

The third concept I relied on was "focusing on the skills." This was a concept that I learned from former U.S. Olympic

Ski Team coach Cooper Schell, who successfully coached American Jonny Moseley to a gold medal at the 1998 Nagano Olympics. Schell taught me that no matter what situation I was in, I could always come back to the skills I spent a lifetime mastering.

I knew in my mind that I had worked harder and longer than any of my competitors to master the skills necessary to be the best in the world, so the idea of turning off my brain and just allowing my body to do what it has been trained to do reduced the amount of mental noise that once existed in my mind. In skiing, that meant reminding myself that my skills would get me down the mountain one hundred percent of the time. In football, it was remembering that my skills would allow me to catch every ball, punt, and kickoff.

We all go through periods in life where we feel a little off or overly nervous. In these moments, it's helpful to bring things back to basics and think about what skills are necessary to accomplish the task at hand.

Even Keeled

One of my all-time favorite quotes is: "Don't allow the good days to go to your head or the bad days to go to your heart." I appreciate this quote because it serves as a constant reminder to always remain balanced no matter what the outcome may be.

One characteristic that I have observed among successful people is their ability to stay even keeled through the highs and lows of life, business, and sport. Michael Jordan and his coach Phil Jackson are famous for their Zen-like approach to life and basketball. John Elway is another person who embodies this trait. John had been a hero of mine basically since the day I was born. My family and I were huge Denver Bronco fans, and I had the privilege of meeting John and becoming friends when I was seventeen. During his sixteen seasons as an NFL quarterback, Elway always remained even keeled. He never seemed unnerved or shaken by what occurred on the field and had a disposition that kept him under control. Perhaps it's due to this reason that John has one of the most fourth quarter comebacks in NFL history.

Passion, Resiliency, and Steve Jobs

Steve Jobs provides an inspiring story of passion, resiliency, and tenacity. If you haven't watched his 2005 commencement address to the graduating class of Stanford University, I encourage you to do so. In it, Jobs, who never graduated from college, talked about the ten-year journey he had taken with his business partner, Steve Wozniak, from a small business in a garage to a $2 billion company with more than 4,000 employees. Passionate about their work, they had succeeded in creating Apple and had released the Macintosh. They were elated. Then, about a year later, Jobs was fired from the company he had founded.

During the commencement speech, he asked the question: "How can you get fired from a company you started? What had been the focus of my entire adult life was gone, and it was devastating," Jobs said. For some time, he felt the pain and guilt of letting others down. He even apologized for "screwing up."

But shortly thereafter came one of the most notable recalibrations in corporate history. "I didn't see it then, but it turned out that getting fired from Apple was the best thing that could have ever happened to me," he says. "The heaviness of being successful was replaced by the lightness of being a beginner again, less sure about everything. It freed me to enter one of the most creative periods of my life."

He took the lessons and wisdom he gleaned from Apple and used them to start NeXT, Inc. and was also part of the founding team that launched Pixar Animation Studios. Today, Pixar is one of the most successful animation studios on the planet. And eventually, Apple acquired NeXT, and Jobs came back to Apple, reviving the company and overseeing the invention of the iPod, iPhone, and iPad. Few people have mastered the art of recalibration better than Steve Jobs.

"Sometimes life hits you in the head with a brick. Don't lose faith," Steve Jobs said. I don't know how long it took Jobs to recalibrate from being fired from his own company, but like others who are steadfast in their desire to succeed, he did so quickly. Moving beyond disappointment does not mean pushing it aside, but rather using it to reprogram the compass of success and continuing the journey.

Planting Seeds

You might think it's easier to use the 48-hour rule and bounce back when you have another goal waiting in the wings, like my goal of making the NFL. And I do believe that is the case. For that reason and many others, I think planting seeds in other areas is an important aspect in creating a long-term plan for yourself. Proactively doing things, especially during times that you have other things going on, is worth the additional effort it requires. Often, these seeds will ultimately grow into what becomes your next journey, but if we don't plant them, they will never grow.

Too many of us put all our eggs in one basket. I can't count the number of times growing up that I heard I should only focus on skiing because I was too small to play football and I might have a better shot at getting to the Olympics if I maintained a single focus. Some coaches wanted me to specialize as early as 12 years old. I didn't listen, and I'm happy I didn't. Coach Barnett taught us to "never leave a stone unturned in life." He encouraged us to always look underneath every aspect of opportunity in our life, no matter how busy or successful we were. That concept is something that has stuck with me, and I have found great value in. I planted a lot of seeds in different areas throughout my athletic journey. Most of them did not grow, but they all taught me great lessons, introduced me to interesting people, and opened my mind to related areas. However, no matter who we are, all of us only have twenty-four hours in a day, and most of us sleep seven to eight of those hours. So, we need to be intentional with how much time we dedicate towards investing in future opportunities. As a rule, somewhere between five and ten percent of our time is a good benchmark.

CHAPTER FOUR
GIVE UP YOUR NEED TO WIN?

Is Winning Everything? For me, it was...for a very long time. After all, I was born into a culture and media landscape that taught me that my heroes should be those with the most wins, people who make the most money and attract the most fame. I wanted to win everything, beat every skier on the planet, win every football game, and be the best player in the world. My concept of winning was defined by what I saw around me: the perks of being a winner. But as I grew older, my definition of winning began to shift. I realized that winning wasn't just about achieving external success, but also about personal growth and fulfillment. I began to understand that true winning was about being the best version of myself and using my talents and abilities to make a positive impact on the world. It's easy to get caught up in the idea that winning is everything, especially in a society that values external success. But it's important to remember that winning is subjective, and that true success is often about personal growth and fulfillment, not just external achievements.

Being focused on winning isn't necessarily bad and let's face it, winning feels a lot better than not. My desire to win helped me in many ways, driving me to train longer, harder, and more intensely than I ever thought possible. But it also hurt me by losing focus, overworking and never being happy. My athletic trainer, Chris Marchetti, would tell you that my biggest blind spot as an athlete was that I consistently overtrained. I wouldn't give my body a chance to recuperate because I was obsessed with having the mental confidence of knowing that I worked harder than everyone else.

For roughly twenty-two years of my life, my ego was the primary driver of my athletic career. I wanted to beat everyone, make all the money and be as famous as possible. But that all changed in the fall of 2004, when my mom gave me a book by Wayne Dyer called *The Power of Intention* before leaving for fall ski team camp.

I took the book with me to South America to train for the World Cup season and dove in. In one section of the book, Dyer talks about giving up the need to win. My first reaction was, "Ha, ha, has this guy lost his mind?" Why would I give up my need to win? That's what has defined my life, motivated me to get this far—it was the foundation of my entire athletic career.

But for some reason the statement stuck with me and kept coming back to me time and time again. It even kept me up at night, and I started to unpack the thought in my head and began questioning whether my desire to win was hurting my ability to in fact win. I reflected on my athletic career and wins and losses along the way. I realized that most of my motivation was extrinsic and hardly any of it was intrinsically driven. All I cared about was beating so-and-so, having everyone like me, making money, and getting attention. But was that making me happy? And did it really help me reach my full potential or was this the reason I landed on my back in that World Cup in France, because my ego couldn't get out of its own way?

After digesting this new information, I became passionate about figuring out ways to remove the motivational control that my ego had on my goals.

But how can you take 22 years of social conditioning and completely reprogram your ego? I started by doing something that made me uncomfortable: helping my biggest competitors. In training, I would mention tips for the course, things like, "Hey, watch out for the last turn before the top jump; it's sharp and icy . . . take it high left and you will be fine." I couldn't believe I was doing this at the time and my competitors surely couldn't believe it either. But it did something magical inside of me; it entirely liberated my intense ego-driven desire to beat other people and replaced it with intrinsic thoughts on what I needed to do to maximize my full and absolute potential as a competitive athlete. Pat Riley, former coach of the New York Knicks, summed it up eloquently: "A champion needs a motivation above and beyond winning. Excellence is the gradual result of always striving to do better."

Letting Go of the Need to Win

To become more intrinsically motivated, I stopped focusing on beating others and caring what everyone thought about me. I began focusing more on what I wanted to get out of life, the person that I ultimately wanted to become, and how I could become the best version of myself. And ironically, I started winning much more often.

The following ski season after reading Dyer's book and putting all my mental fortitude into becoming an intrinsically driven athlete, I won more consecutive world cup races than anyone in the sport's history.

But the feeling of winning this time was much different. I wasn't excited because I beat other people; I was simply pleased that I skied up to my full potential. I won my second consecutive World Cup event that year and remember thinking to myself that I wouldn't lose the rest of the year. I was competing with perfect mental clarity which allowed my body to do what it had trained how to do nearly every day of my life. The ego-driven thoughts of beating anyone else was completely gone. I even found myself listening to classical music before an event rather than the loud punk rock that I used to listen to before a race. When I won my fourth and fifth consecutive World Cup events, more and more people began approaching me to talk about the record. Although I never told them, I found myself slightly annoyed by the conversations because I truly didn't care about breaking any records. Only the ego would care about something so trivial. Nonetheless, after winning a record-breaking six consecutive world cup races, I allowed myself to indulge in a glass of celebratory champagne.

It's remarkable what a big impact that one chapter in an otherwise seemingly inconsequential book had on my life. But it's true after reading Dyer's book and committing to doing the hard work to reprogram my ego, I became the best version of myself and was able to maximize my full potential. People often ask how dominate athletes get into "the zone." Reprogramming my ego to focus intrinsically was how I did it.

Can a person be totally intrinsically motivated?

"Not necessarily; it's not always black and white," says Brad Feld, partner at the Boulder, Colorado-based venture capital firm Foundry Group. I consider Brad a good friend and someone who has helped me better understand the difference between intrinsic and extrinsic motivation. I met Brad through a good friend, Bing Gordon, the co-founder of EA Sports, and we quickly became friends. His firm was also the first investor in my startup, Integrate. As he explains, "People fall along a continuum."

Brad uses tennis star Rafael Nadal as an example. He sees Nadal as having a blend of both extrinsic and intrinsic motivation. Nadal clearly likes to win. He likes the limelight and the attention he gets. "Yet . . . Nadal, after he loses a match, he is very gracious, acknowledging that the other guy played better and did an awesome job."

Nadal recharges his battery by heading off to the beach, and then he is back in training for the next tournament. His daily training regime includes four hours of playing tennis on court, two and a half hours in the gym, and a strict stretching routine. He's continued this training whether he is ranked at number one, five, or seven in the world. It's for him, not for the ranking.

Brad also believes something I've really taken to heart—that one person can't truly motivate another person, a concept especially important in business if you're a manager. "I can't motivate another person, but [I can] create a context in which they are motivated, and part of being a leader is to understand what motivates other people," explained Brad. "So if I'm the leader of an organization that you're a part of, I have to understand what motivates you. Then I can create a context in which to motivate you. Most people struggle to understand how somebody else is motivated because they do it based on what motivates them."

Ultimately, gaining knowledge is a main satisfaction driver for intrinsically motivated people. Albert Einstein talked about intrinsic motivation as "the enjoyment of seeing and searching." Health, fitness, and well-being—physical and mental—are also frequently mentioned in studies as being among the most significant internal motivations. Personal satisfaction can also come from skills enhancement, along with enlightenment, understanding, reconciling, and self-discovery. But how can we identify and apply elements of motivation in our daily lives? How can we establish new behaviors or modify existing ones, so they become natural extensions of ourselves?

Workplace Motivators

Another book I enjoyed reading is *Enemies of Exploration: Self-Initiated vs. Other-Initiated Learning*, by John Condry. In the book, John suggests that one should "Choose a job you love, and you will never have to work a day in your life."

Taking the work out of work is very appealing, yet not always easy to achieve. To begin with, most people struggle to know for sure what their biggest passion is and how they could turn that into a profession. I like to think that if you enjoy your job 50 percent of the time, you are incredibly lucky.

Finding purpose in our professional careers beyond the paycheck is crucial to find broader meaning in our work. The sense of personal pride we get from excelling at what we do, taking actions to help our fellow colleagues, working to improve the overall culture, and sharing ideas how the company can improve to senior management are all ways to build inner satisfaction and reinforce intrinsic motivating forces.

Building self-satisfaction in the workplace has been shown in numerous studies to result in improved company culture and greater individual and/or team productivity. Although, motivation and job satisfaction are highly subjective. For example, one person may feel greater satisfaction being responsible for making important decisions and leading projects, while another may be more comfortable in a supporting role. Personal motivation and desire differ from one person to another. But what I believe is most important is that everyone feels empowered to be the CEO of their job, no matter how big or small their title or seniority at the company.

J. K. Rowling was motivated to write the Harry Potter books because she was simply trying to create stories to read to her children. Her driving motivation was not to make billions of dollars. Some of the best ideas and businesses are born out of a passion that starts small and grows over time.

Take Uber for example; their first goal was to create a ride sharing program in San Francisco only. They hyper focused on making this one city work before they expanded all over the world.

Intrinsic motivation also works in team situations if each team member respects and understands his or her own role and the roles of others. It's about focusing on the team's efforts and not on the competition or on getting your own individual praise. If nobody needs to be the star, then everyone can give their all to the team. As legendary UCLA basketball coach John Wooden said, "It is amazing how much can be accomplished if no one cares who gets the credit."

CHAPTER FIVE
THE ROADMAP FOR RECALIBRATION

We all go through many seasons of change in our lives and oftentimes they can be worrisome because the evolutionary human spirt thrives on predictability. And change is anything but predictable. During my athletic career I frequently struggled with wondering what would I do when my days of competing as a pro ended. Would I have any skills that would translate into the workplace? Would anyone even consider hiring me? Would I find passion and purpose?

These were my biggest fears as an athlete. I never feared getting injured. I wasn't afraid of not achieving my goals. I wasn't afraid of not living up to expectations. It was what came next that worried me. I had seen countless teammates leave sports and move into the "real world" with little or no plan in place for their future. They often ended up struggling to find their way and became meaningfully depressed. I was determined to do everything in my power to make sure that didn't happen in my life but there was absolutely no guarantee.

I needed a road map, or at least a map with some clear points of interest. So, I dove in and began planting seeds for a possible future career path. Most of these seeds—everything from real estate ventures to various business plans—never grew. But two seeds ended up growing into a bigger passion that I could have ever imagined, and both were created from my own personal road map.

When we first started Integrate, we had little idea what the product would ultimately become. But we experimented often and were relentless in our pursuit to find product market fit. As is most often the case with young startups, that typically happens through trial and error.

Consider the story of Tony Bates, who I first met at an Olympic fundraiser at The Yellowstone Club in Big Sky, Montana. Tony worked directly for John Chambers, the legendary chairman of the board and CEO at Cisco. After 14 years at Cisco, Bates became the CEO of Skype and led the company through an $8.5 billion acquisition by Microsoft. After joining Microsoft, Tony was one of the tech company's top choices to succeed former CEO Steve Ballmer when he stepped down. When he wasn't chosen, Tony left and went on to become president of GoPro. Perhaps this doesn't seem unusual, as CEOs do move around. But what I love about Tony's story is that he told me that he set in writing his intention to become the CEO of Skype while he was still at

Cisco. He wrote down the names of three companies where he would someday become CEO and Skype was one of them. Talk about manifesting your destiny.

As I mentioned earlier, when I was ten years old, I told my mom and dad that I wanted to ski in the Olympics and get drafted into the NFL. I also mentioned that I needed to get my college degree as a backup plan in case neither of those things panned out (shout-out to my mom). Both of my parents have a healthy disrespect for the impossible so after I told them my goals they said, "You can accomplish both if you put your mind to it and attack your dreams." I defined what I wanted to accomplish, dedicated the effort, and made it happen.

The Time Is Now

"I may come across as someone who is heavily biased towards taking action, and you would be correct. However, there are times when I struggle to initiate the things that I truly desire. During such moments, I remind myself that each passing day is a reminder that time is slipping away from me. Today is the youngest that we will ever be. With this realization, I am motivated to prioritize the things that matter to me the most.

We only have a limited time on this beautiful planet, and to make the most of it, we must embrace our inherent bias towards action. As the famous quote goes, "Don't talk about it, be about it." Let us seize the day and take action towards realizing our goals and living a fulfilling life."

When I was playing with the Philadelphia Eagles, I learned about an NFL continuing education program where you could take MBA level classes at Kellogg, Harvard,

Stanford, or Wharton. Since I was living just outside of Philadelphia, I thought it would be a great stone to unturn and see what I could learn and how I could be inspired.

The NFL ended up impacting my life more off the field than on it. The Wharton program inspired me in similar ways to how the Olympics touched my soul as a young child. I became friends with one of my professors, Peter Linnemen, a legendary real estate investor and Wharton instructor for many years. Peter allowed me to visit his office after practice and work with him and his team at American Land Fund. ALF was a private equity company that purchased land in notoriously difficult entitlement counties. It would then work with the county to get proper development titles and flip the land to big developers for a massive profit. This experience really opened my eyes to the capital markets and served as a first entry point to learn how to raise money from other investors—something that would pay huge dividends when I took to the venture capital fundraising trail for Integrate.

The great thing about books and online classes is that no matter what problem you might be struggling with, there has already been another human who figured out how to solve it. We just must look deeply enough for the right book, class or keynote.

I also think that remaining intellectually curious throughout our whole life is critical to our own development as humans. Many colleges and universities offer short, intensive courses or part-time classes that meet weekly. There are also numerous online courses that can cost as little as a few hundred dollars per semester. These can be great ways to test something you are passionate about. Coursera.org, for example, has thousands of courses available from some of the finest universities in the world, including Princeton and Stanford.

For me, I knew I was interested in entrepreneurship, but I didn't know how to build a company from scratch. Once I began learning about internet startups and how they worked, I became hooked fast. My passion for having my own startup grew quickly after I completed my work at Wharton and I began to notice a passion shift in my life away from sports and more towards starting a business.

Most of the big changes in my life have been preceded by an intentional effort to plant new seeds. However, rarely did anything grow overnight; it took many months and sometimes years to see which new areas of opportunity would lead me in the direction of my next adventure.

Passion + Need = Business Opportunity

Shortly after my NFL career ended, I decided to join a company that a new friend was building called Mdinfo. Working at the company gave me my first opportunity to learn about digital marketing, lead generation and the challenge every company faces to win more customers.

The goal of MDinfo was to build a global social network of doctors, nurses, and healthcare professionals to share their knowledge in a personal way with consumers. WebMD had captured most of the market share in the healthcare content category, but we believed that there was a need for a way for people to have a more personalized experience with healthcare experts on the web. We wanted to build a cadre of experts to help people—helping those experts build their own brands in the process. It was a traditional marketplace business, but those can be the hardest to succeed in because managing the supply and demand on both sides is tricky. If you have too much demand and not enough supply, users won't get their health questions answered and likely would never come back. If you had too much supply but not enough demand the health care professional wouldn't see enough impact on the time they invested answering questions.

At the peak, Mdinfo captured around 90 million unique visitors from more than 36 countries in one month. We didn't sell display ads because very few healthcare companies wanted their ads to appear next to user-generated content that they have no control over. Instead, we monetized by helping companies generate new leads for their products and services. When a consumer asked a question in a specific healthcare category, they could opt for different deals and products in that category.

One of the biggest pain points we encountered led to the creation of Integrate. All our marketing systems were disconnected and none of them meaningfully connected to the others. This led to millions of dollars of marketing inefficiencies. We had to hire numerous people to manually pull data to and from various systems and use an Excel spreadsheet to try and make sense of it all. And the problem got bigger and more costly as the company grew.

We couldn't find a product on the market that integrated all the channels and the lead data into one platform, so we started building one. We thought that if it worked, we could potentially save Mdinfo more than $350,000 per month, while increasing engagement rates on the site by 30 percent. And it did work and opened our eyes to a much larger market opportunity.

My co-founder and I realized that if we solved the primary pain point of marketing departments everywhere, this company could be worth many billions of dollars. We had such conviction that we turned our focus to building out this technology and Integrate was born.

Recalibrations in Business

The best startups are nimble and thrive on the art of recalibration, especially in those early forming years. Many great household name businesses started out doing something completely different than they do today. Take Groupon for example; this company started off as an online collective action and fundraising platform before pivoting into the social commerce space.

There are many stories of major pivots in well-known businesses. A few examples:

1. Flickr was a role-playing gaming site for a couple years before emerging as the popular photo-sharing social media site.
2. Apple started out selling computer kits to kids before making their own computers and emerging as a $700 billion business.
3. Lego started by making wooden ducks. A few years after a fire burned down the factory,

management decided to switch to plastic toys, and what emerged? The interlocking bricks that have spawned a multibillion-dollar business that encompasses TV shows, movies, creation contests, and more.

4. Nokia began as a paper mill and expanded into making rubber goods before moving to electronics and eventually to mobile phones.

5. Avon was started by a door-to-door book salesman who gave away free samples of perfume. The perfume got better reviews than the books, so he did a complete pivot and dumped the books in favor of starting the California Perfume Company, a precursor of Avon.

Another great story of recalibration comes from Eric Roza. After several years in various businesses, Eric, a friend of mine, in January 2007 joined a company called NextAction. At the time, the company helped small retail businesses target their catalogs to intended shoppers. It was based on predictive analytics, which meant bringing together a lot of data and then building statistical models to figure out the likelihood of a customer being interested in a catalog from a given retailer.

"In 2007 and 2008, if your only business was targeting print catalogs you knew you had problems since the catalog market was not exactly growing," Eric explained to me. The company took a major hit soon after when the United States Postal Service levied what was roughly a 40 percent increase in the cost of postage for catalogs.

"We were now relying entirely on print catalogs in a digital world with increasing postage. Before we knew it, the business was literally plummeting into oblivion," Eric recounted. He was second in command at the company at the time and was later asked to be CEO. "We were declining by 40 percent a year and we didn't know where the bottom was. My first action as CEO was to cut my own salary by 20 percent along with the salaries of the other 110 employees, which was far better than layoffs," Eric told me. He says he wouldn't have accepted the helm if he hadn't already been an executive at the company.

It was also around this time that the company started building and investing in an online model. That idea came from the belief that the kind of data being gathered—information about what people had purchased in the past—was the kind of data that would be valuable online. The concept was to provide such information to advertisers who would want to focus on what people had purchased before, rather than focusing on what they were reading about or what they were saying they would purchase.

For a year the business struggled, defaulting on its bank covenants, and finding no sympathy with existing investors who no longer wanted to put any more money into the company. Eric describes the situation as having been "quite tense, especially with the board of directors."

"This was a company that was very successful in the past on a small scale, so expectations had been set high," recalls Eric. "But the company was now worth almost nothing by late 2008." He knew he had to raise money at any cost, take it on the chin, and figure out how much or how little the company was worth. That's a tough spot to be in. "At the end of the day, we needed to generate new capital and we needed to have a board [of directors] that believed in the vision that I had for the company. If they did not believe in what we were trying to do, I knew the situation was futile."

Roza reached out to General Catalyst, a leading venture capital firm, whose executive-in-residence, Rob Gierkink, and founder, David Fialkow, agreed to fund the company's digital future. NextAction was rebranded as Datalogix in October of 2009—and became one of the most significant companies in the world of digital advertising. With its aggregated data about customer purchasing from 1,500 sources, the company successfully went after major online clients such as Facebook, Google, Twitter, and Yahoo!.

And that proved to be a turning point—a new direction on the road map. "Our data had to be everywhere so it could benefit advertisers," explained Eric. "If a big consumer brand like Kraft or Chrysler decided to advertise, they wouldn't know if the ads were driving the product or not, because 94 percent of the sales are offline—so we became the guys who connected the dots for the big advertisers and big digital publishers." Datalogix became the link between the advertising and what customers were buying in stores or at car dealers.

And guess what? Eric's plan worked. He led a major pivot and took a company from the brink of disaster, in a new "digital" direction. Today, Datalogix—recently bought out by Oracle for $1.2 billion—works with 80 of the top

100 brands in America and is a leader in its field. Ironically, thanks to its infusion of new data and hiring of dozens of the country's best data scientists, even the company's legacy catalog business experienced a renaissance and continues to grow.

CHAPTER SIX
RECALIBRATING A NEW PATH

The toughest part about starting off in a new career is the fear of the unknown. You are suddenly the newcomer, like a new kid at school all over again, wondering how things are going to play out. For me, the toughest part of redefining myself as an entrepreneur was that it was all new to me, back on the bunny hill learning to ski all over again.

One of the biggest reasons professional athletes go broke after their playing days are over is because they don't have solid mentors who can help them navigate the complex world of investing. They often make poor choices and invest in losing assets. Wharton professor Peter Linneman's advice to me was before I spent my own capital to start a business that I should, "go lose someone else's money first" by joining a startup and learning.

A New Challenge

When I left athletics, my goal was to completely redefine myself. I wanted to climb a mountain that was entirely new to me. I was energized to try something new, to step into a different arena, with different rules, different players, and different unforeseen challenges. People in the new space might already know you, as was my case. But even so, those connections knew me as an athlete. I didn't know how they would react to me now as an entrepreneur. Would they see me as the ill-equipped former athlete? Would they embrace my ideas?

One of the biggest challenges when embarking on a new career is controlling your own psychology. Essentially, you must be mentally comfortable feeling uncomfortable. Chances are, you've spent a great amount of time in your life working toward, and maybe reaching, a goal. It is understandable that you will be uncomfortable starting again; transitions are scary, but they are also the moments when we feel the most alive. When Steve Jobs was fired from Apple, it was a mentally challenging experience, but he recounted it as a time in his life when he felt most alive.

For me, after dedicating most of my life to football and skiing, I was excited to start over at the bottom of a new and exciting mountain.

Apolo Ohno, a good friend of mine, is best known for his eight Olympic speed skating medals (two gold, two silver, and four bronze) at three separate winter Olympic Games—not to mention his 21 medals at the World Championships. But he's also amid making a post-sports transition. He knows that apprehension that many of us feel all too well.

"Making such a transition for an athlete is never easy; it doesn't matter how much money you amassed or how successful you were," Apolo tells me. "When you've spent your entire life focused solely on one thing, it's hard to refocus. The transition is usually painful and difficult for an athlete."

Coming Full Circle

When she was in college, Gail Sagel's father asked her what she planned to do for a career. She explained that with people living longer, she saw a need for an anti-aging approach to skin care and makeup. Her father looked at her, shook his head, and told her she should go to law school or business school. She dutifully followed her father's advice and went on to work on Wall Street after graduating from the University of Maryland School of Business, double majoring in economics and marketing.

During college, Gail interned with First Options of Chicago, where she learned how to trade options on the floor of the American Stock exchange. Soon, she was working for Bear Stearns in the United States and abroad. While working with clients in Paris, France, she would spend her downtime visiting spas and observing cosmetic trends at the makeup counters of Le Bon Marche and the Galeries Lafayette. For Gail, these excursions were a much-needed break from the many hours spent in a cutthroat trading environment with a cast of characters that she likened to those in the movie *The Wolf of Wall Street*, and at the time, in the late 1980s, most of her colleagues were male. In 1993, after Gail gave birth to twins, she resigned after struggling to find good child-care options.

Five years later, with her children entering grade school and her marriage over, Gail, now living in Connecticut, needed to return to work. The culture of the financial industry had changed since she'd been out of it, and so had the finance opportunities in Connecticut, where many hedge funds had set up shop. Gail was able to find work at a small Connecticut firm. Yet she was still doing something she didn't feel passionate about. Then one day, while biking home from work, she was hit by a car.

In the ambulance, Gail recalls thinking the accident was a sign that she needed to change her life. Following a full recovery, Gail was reminded, by her best college girlfriend, of her long-time passion for makeup and just how good she had been at performing makeovers. In 1999, she opened FACES Beautiful, starting in her living room and developing into a luxury makeup studio, upscale salon, and beauty boutique in Connecticut. Gail had come full circle from her earliest passions all the way back to what she loved to do. She had been very successful in the financial world. She had not failed, but the environment in that industry had failed her.

Sometimes, failure isn't from the efforts of the individual but from a toxic environment from which you need to escape. Now, more than 15 years later, the studio continues to be successful, and Gail has created a makeup and a skincare brand which are sold nationally online.

Passion can be found at any age—and rediscovered if you left it behind.

As an athlete whose goal is often to become the best in the world, "your career path in life is magnified and you usually don't have time to do anything else," Apolo told me—and I can relate. "Some people find the time to go to school, but for the most part, at that level of commitment, you simply cannot afford to diversify your life very much." For athletes, making change is even harder because the level of adrenaline in athletics, especially at the peak level, is high, and "we're constantly searching for the same kind of stimuli."

That's not easy, as both Apolo and I—and countless others—have found.

It's never easy to find the time, whether in sports or in business, to find a new venture to explore, much less gain some knowledge and experience in that area of interest. For someone who's spent years in the fast-paced, competitive world of finance, it can be quite eye-opening to suddenly find yourself slowly trying to build a business as a new entrepreneur.

Taking Something with You

For anyone changing careers, it's easier to move to something new when you realize you can take something with you from your first act.

In his career transition, for instance, Apolo says he learned "to apply aspects of sports, such as how to train and how I represented myself during the Olympic games. My goal was to take those same attributes and apply them toward business opportunities, whether it was in broadcasting, the tech industry, natural resources, supplements and nutraceuticals, clothing, or brokering deals."

Apolo says he tried to find a similar path as he did when he was skating and apply the same sort of focus and competitive training-oriented mindset to whatever came next. "Of course, I realized that it was not going to be as instantaneous as my sport, where a race lasted 40 seconds, but I'm always looking to improve and to see where I can go from here," he says. "That's what drives me."

Keys to Changing Careers

Whether you are walking away from a business that didn't work, a dream that did not come true, or a successful career where you accomplished your goals, it's a good idea to dedicate some time to exploring other ideas. One of them could eventually lead you to the next chapter of your professional career. Even during my athletic careers, when almost every second of my day was allocated to training or competing, I would find time to explore future possibilities and ideas.

Besides finding something that you enjoy, consider taking the time to research a new area of interest. Many successful leaders put a lot of time into staying current in their industry and reading everything they can to understand the space and learn about the competition.

When starting Integrate, we needed to know whether we were entering a growing market or a saturated one. We needed to know if there was a market for our product, how big that market was (and the growth potential), and whether we had significant competition. Reading and studying then, and now, was and is vital to our success. You may be passionate about starting a specific type of business, but based on your due diligence, the timing might not be right. If that's the case, you will either need to be patient, modify your product or idea, or explore some of the other seeds you have planted.

Networking Through LinkedIn

A great place for networking is in the social media—and particularly LinkedIn. The thing that I use LinkedIn the most for now is finding talented people who might be interested in joining Integrate. It is easy to search by company name, job title, and level of experience.

A few other ways to utilize the site:

- The advanced feature on top of your profile page shows the connections of your connections by category—you can then ask your connections if they are okay with you reaching out to their connections.

- Join groups in your area of business and join the conversation or start a thread with a thought-provoking question; respond privately with people you think you'd like to add to your network.

- Stay current. Update your profile page, share current news, and update and link to your own blog often. If you have a premium account, you can also use Open Link to send messages to people to whom you are not yet connected.

- Read what your connections are sharing and responding to. Let people know you are paying attention to their news and information.
- It's also important to open doors and grab people's attention. Give them something unique or provocative (yet professional).

Once you've found your way, the most successful people never stop studying. Proven entrepreneurs, like Tony Bates of Genesys, continue monitoring their industry every single day.

It's also important to expand your network from the start. It can be intimidating at first, trying to connect with people you might not know. But social media—especially LinkedIn—has made reaching out to new business contacts easier than ever. LinkedIn is a great tool to connect with people who can be a resource for you when you start looking into a new idea. You might be surprised to find that you already have more contacts than you think.

Along with meeting people on LinkedIn through groups or mutual connections, I also find it fascinating and inspirational to talk with people who are way ahead of me, with years of experience. People who have "been there and done that" are often willing to share a lot of their wisdom with you. Some of those people, whose opinions, and suggestions I regard very highly, have become advisors and mentors of mine in life, work, and this book. I always look to hire people who have learned through making mistakes on someone else's balance sheet.

Successful Transitions

In 2012, I was asked by Young Presidents Organization (YPO), a global network of young chief executives, to give a keynote talk at their annual ski trip to Squaw Valley, California. David Karnstedt was one of the first people that I met there. He had recently sold his software advertising company, Efficient Frontier, to Adobe for $400 million, and because we were both building companies in a similar space, we had a lot to talk about. Today, David serves on Integrate's board of advisors and is someone for whom I have a tremendous amount of respect.

Among the most inspiring things about David: He discovered a passion in a career he hated and transformed it into an industry that he enjoyed.

"I sold surgical equipment once upon a time, working from my home," he says. "My office was essentially every hospital in the Midwest. I hated that job. I didn't fail at it—in fact, I won rookie of the year at a sales conference. Then I quit," says David, who wasn't happy in surgical sales. However, there was something about the work that he did love. He was in medical sales at the time when arthroscopic and endoscopic surgery were becoming popular, and David discovered he had a real passion for the technology involved. "I loved this stuff. I just needed to find a job in another industry," explains David, and he did just that. He later went on to run North American sales for Yahoo! And become CEO of Efficient Frontier.

Finding a passion makes transitioning into a new career infinitely more interesting. For athletes and some others, the need for a second passion is so important because a career can be so fleeting.

Roger Staubach's Dual Success Story

If you remember watching Roger Staubach play quarterback for Navy or in the NFL for the Dallas Cowboys, I envy you. I'm too young to have ever seen Staubach play, but I know that he was a Heisman Trophy winner in 1963, then served in the Navy in Vietnam, returning to have an 11-year career with the Dallas Cowboys, taking them to four Super Bowls and winning two of them. Staubach won a Most Valuable P layer award and made the Pro Bowl six times in the 1970s.

He is also someone I greatly admire because he transitioned from being a Hall-of-Fame quarterback to building an amazing career in real estate. Perhaps the most interesting aspect of Staubach's transition is that unlike so many athletes, me included, he did not wait until after football to plant seeds in hopes of finding something to do. Instead, he planted them, learned a business, and immersed himself in it *while* playing football.

"When I came out of the Naval Academy in 1965, I had a four-year obligation to the service, and we had three children that were born while in the Navy. In those days, they didn't pay quarterbacks what they do today, and as a 27-year-old rookie with a wife and three children, I was thinking that if I got hurt and couldn't play, I would need to have something else I could fall back on," Staubach recounts. "So, in the off-season I interviewed with a couple of companies and went to work for a Texas real estate firm that was going to pay me on commission. This was a good deal because I could only work there half of the year, but if I were productive, I would get rewarded. What was also good was that I could learn about the real estate industry while I was still playing." Staubach worked for, and learned from, Henry S. Miller, who mentored him at what was the largest independent commercial real estate firm in the state.

According to Staubach, there were many things that he could transfer from sports into business. Among them: teamwork, perseverance, and hard work. He has said, "It takes a lot of unspectacular preparation to have spectacular results in both business and football."

Staubach says real estate was a good career move in part because he also enjoyed the competitive side of the business. In a short time, it became a passion. "It's a very competitive industry, and that was something I liked about real estate. That made it challenging and interesting for me," says Staubach, who in 1979 teamed with broker Robert Holloway to form the Holloway-Staubach Corporation. Yes, that was two years before he retired from the NFL and only a few months before he led the Cowboys to victory in Super Bowl XII over the Denver Broncos.

"After 11 seasons, I had six concussions where I was totally knocked out and I was 38 years old. I was coming off a really good season, and our general manager, Tex Schramm, wanted me to play two more years. In fact, he offered me one of the biggest contracts ever at that time," recalls Staubach. But his doctor had other ideas. "He told me that I'd had too many [concussions] and the next one could be serious. So, I decided to pursue my life after football and retired from the game to take on the challenge of building my company."

The lessons he took from sports served him well in his new career in business. "Like sports, you have to have the right people in the right places, and they have to work well together," he says. "I worked hard at bringing in a lot of good people. I devoted enough time and energy to the real estate business so that people knew I was committed to it. They knew I wasn't just an athlete putting my name on the door."

In time, Staubach bought out Holloway and the company expanded from a Texas real estate firm into a major national real estate company, winning many major contracts globally.

In 2008, the Staubach Company was sold to Jones Lang LaSalle for $613 million. Staubach currently serves as executive chairman of Jones Lang LaSalle. He is considered by many to be the most successful superstar athlete turned entrepreneur. He also truly epitomizes the concept of planting seeds, starting out under someone else before investing your own money, and following your passions.

I love Roger Staubach's story of success. He was prescriptive about learning a new skill while he was still playing professional athletics, and like Wharton professor Peter Linnemen suggests, he worked for a real estate firm first before starting his own business. In an era where athletes are making more money than in the days of Roger Staubach, we can test the waters a little more carefully.

Yet, that can also backfire, as many former athletes expect many doors to open after sports simply because of their name and their previous success. They sometimes face a rude awakening when that does not happen. At the Olympic level, and even for successful athletes coming out of the NCAA, there is a time when you are not sure what comes next in life. It's easy to get immersed in sports, from the dedication and the excitement that comes with it, but hard to see what will come next.

CHAPTER SEVEN
LEADERSHIP, CHEMISTRY, AND VICTIMS

One of the things that struck me about the culture of the Steelers was the emphasis on team harmony and unity. This was in stark contrast to the fear-based culture that I had experienced with the Eagles, where players were constantly worried about being cut.

I came to realize that fear was not an effective motivator in the long term. Instead, it seemed to breed anxiety and insecurity, which could ultimately undermine team cohesion and performance. On the other hand, a culture of harmony and support seemed to foster greater resilience and cooperation, leading to more success on the field.

As I began to formulate my own management style in the years following my football career, these experiences stayed with me. I tried to cultivate an environment that was supportive and collaborative, rather than one that relied on fear as a motivator. And while I can't claim to have always gotten it right, I believe that this approach has helped me to build more successful teams and organizations in my business endeavors.

Managing Your Team: Top-Down or Bottom-Up?

Top-down management, as the name suggests, means that all decision-making and direction in business or sports originates from the top and cascades down to the next level of managers or coaches, and then to the team. While this style has proven effective in some industries, it can also alienate team members who feel that their opinions and input are not valued. Top-down management can also lead to a lack of motivation among employees because they do not feel ownership or input in their work and the goals of the company, which often leads to reduced productivity. On the other hand, the bottom-up approach to management is gaining popularity because it allows people to feel that their opinions are heard and valued.

In such environments, team members feel more connected to the company's mission and empowered to influence outcomes rather than blame management for any inefficiencies within the business. I experienced both styles of management during my time in the NFL. My first experience was with the Philadelphia Eagles under head coach Andy Reid, a highly committed and knowledgeable coach. With the Eagles, a strict top-down management style dominated with fear-based motivation. In team meetings and player position meetings, coaches would often say things like, "If you don't do XYZ, you're out of here. We'll find someone to replace you; there are plenty of other players out there." Coaches used fear as a means of motivation for the players, but this type of motivation created a disconnected culture within the locker room. It felt like many players were on their own, looking over their shoulders, wondering if they would be the next one to get cut. As a result, players looked out for themselves, and as a team, it hindered our ability to build connectivity. Despite the Eagles having a roster with arguably more talent than the Steelers, the Eagles had yet to win a Super Bowl at the time.

My other experience, with the Pittsburgh Steelers, was completely different. The Rooney family has owned the team for decades and it is a family-oriented organization where everyone is treated with respect. Mike Tomlin, at the time in his second year as head coach, fit this family mentality and led a bottom-up management style very well. He was the best leader I have ever been around. His ability to unify a group of men from different economic, religious, and racial backgrounds, and with a range of individual personality quirks and strengths, was something I had never seen before. Coach Tomlin made you feel like you were part of the Steelers family. He was firm, honest, and at times brutally transparent. It was a locked-arms culture and the most connected locker room I have ever seen. Coach Tomlin allowed you to fail, if you failed fast and quickly corrected it. This was in 2008, the year the Pittsburgh Steelers won their record-setting sixth Super Bowl championship in eight appearances. I believe that the Steelers' success is due in large part to the type of management, leadership, and motivation that are all key ingredients to building a great culture. There was a significant difference in the two environments I played in and experienced during my time in the NFL, and I believe that it impacted the final results.

As a founder and CEO, I try to follow the Steelers' way of management – fully transparent, bottom-up, and respectful of all involved. I know I appreciated working in that environment, and people who are aligned with our cultural mold appreciate it as well. While Andy Reid has had great success as a coach, the Steelers' approach to management and leadership has consistently produced successful results. In business.

The Keys to Building a Strong Team

It's essential to seek out individuals who possess leadership qualities from the outset, according to Laszlo Bock, senior vice president of people operations at Google. This doesn't necessarily mean selecting only those who have previously held positions as presidents of chess clubs or Scout troops, but rather individuals who can step up and take charge when necessary. These individuals, who demonstrate the ability to lead when needed, are highly valued in a leadership culture.

Finding A Partner: The Art Of Co-founding

Another way to move in a new direction is by joining forces with someone else. The truth is, businesses are never the work of just one person. Behind all notable business success stories is a partner of some kind, whether or not that person shares the spotlight, takes the credit, or addresses the media. I think the biggest mistake first-time founders make, which is also quite common, is to choose a best friend as a co-founder or business partner, without considering whether that friend possesses a complementary skill set.

My co-founder at Integrate, who moved on to other ventures in 2014, complemented my blind spots well. His skill set was building technology quickly and efficiently, while mine was in leadership, business development, and sales. Sometimes you'll figure out what you lack early on and seek out people with the talents and skills you need. That's the ideal, of course. But more often in a new business, one partner tries to take on responsibilities they really don't have the skills to handle. And that rarely works out.

It's a good idea to ensure that you know what each founder brings to the table in advance and sort out what needs to be done to compensate for any shortcomings either of you might have. For example, if your partner is introverted and does not handle social situations very well, you will need to either assume more of the social role or discuss ways to make it easier for the two of you as a team to handle social situations.

Of course, it's more than just personality attributes and technical or tactical skills that you need to identify and make fit with co-founders or partners, it's also an unyielding belief in the business, its goals, and, generally, how to achieve them. You need to be aligned and ready to go to bat for each other. It's not that there won't be bumps in the relationship, but your partnership will last longer if you have a similar outlook on how things should be done. With that in mind, it's best to enter a business partnership with someone you know (or get to know) reasonably well. The business environment will throw plenty of challenges in your direction, so it's a good idea to have a similar plan for handling them.

Finally, it's crucial to develop a conflict resolution plan. That might sound silly—especially after you've found a partner with complementary skills and personality traits. Why do you need a conflict resolution plan? Because conflict happens and you cannot let it derail your partnership and your business. Of course, if you bring every issue, you have a disagreement over to the table, you're going to kill the cadence and productivity.

The first couple of years, my co-founder and I had a difficult time figuring out how to have healthy conflicts. We went through one period of conflict that was so bad that we didn't talk to each other for months at a time. I hated it, and it created major challenges in our business. What we worked out after a lot of trial and error was a rating system of discomfort. If either of us felt strongly about something, we would say, "I think this is a bad idea because XYZ, and it's a ten out of ten feeling of discomfort." We agreed that when one of us felt so strongly about something, we would accept that person's point of view and move on. It didn't always work, but it greatly helped us improve our ability to efficiently get past times of disagreement.

The key is to look for the yellow flags and set aside some time to talk about potential issues before they become red flags. In situations where your approach to business is fundamentally different, which my partner and I had at times, you will need to address the situation. If you try working around yellow flags for too long, they will likely become red flags.

Compromise is very important, but even when you do compromise, not every partnership can or will work out. Too many potential red flags early in the process might mean that this partnership is ill-advised, so keep your eyes open for those hints, which could be as simple as X or more complex, like X, Y, and Z.

But as Bock emphasizes, strong team members also need to step back and relinquish power when necessary. Bock says it's important to hire people who are strong-minded and vigorously support their positions, "arguing like hell when necessary." But these same people ought to be able to, when provided with new information, step back and say, "Okay, you're right." As Bock puts it, "You need a big ego and small ego in the same person at the same time."

Such people are hard to find. In sports, or business, these are the people you can give the ball to time after time, but when the defense or business strategies change, they can accept that someone else may need to carry the ball for a while. Unselfish leaders are the ultimate hire when building a strong team.

Other characteristics that I believe are key to building a strong team in business:

1. *A good cultural fit.* I'll take a good culture fit over someone who is highly competent but a

culture risk. As we'll discuss in the next chapter, cultural risks, people who don't want to join the "team" mindset, can bring down the morale of the entire team.

2. *People who don't get in their own way.* There are people who love their own ideas so much that they can't accept that someone else might have a better plan of action. Their own ego can get in the way of a management team moving forward. A common piece of important advice I hear from entrepreneurs of large companies is that as you scale up, make sure you don't have a management team that gets in the way of each other. If you have too many people who love their own ideas too much and don't know when to step back, you start running on a treadmill.

3. *Humility.* If someone can be humble, own up to a mistake or a failed attempt at something, accept criticism and move forward constructively as part of a team, this is a big plus. People who can be humble can get stuff done, and, more than that, they are great team players.

Five Team-Building Quotes That Inspire

"The strength of the team is each individual member. The strength of each member is the team."
—PHIL JACKSON, FORMER COACH OF THE CHAMPIONSHIP CHICAGO BULLS AND L.A. LAKERS

"To be successful, you have to be out there, you have to hit the ground running, and if you have a good team around you and more than a fair share of luck, you might make something happen."
—SIR RICHARD BRANSON, FOUNDER OF THE VIRGIN GROUP LTD.

"A group becomes a team when each member is sure enough of himself and his contribution to praise the skills of others."
—NORMAN SHIDLE, AUTHOR OF SEVERAL BUSINESS AND COMMUNICATION BOOKS

"Your end goal is what can we do together to problem-solve? I've contributed my piece, and then I step back."
—LASZLO BOCK, SENIOR VICE PRESIDENT OF PEOPLE OPERATIONS AT GOOGLE

"I' good players is easy. I' 'em to play together is the hard part."
—CASEY STENGEL, MAJOR LEAGUE MANAGER OF THE NEW YORK YANKEES FOR EIGHT WORLD TITLES

Leaders vs. Victims

Culture starts with building the team, which means evaluating people, and not just by their skillset, or their resume, or even their previous experience. You need to be able to assess who a person really is—their personality, their characteristics, and even their passions and how they will fit in with the mission, goals, and objectives.

The best way that I have found to do this is to conduct thorough back-channel reference checks. I'm not talking about the three or four people the candidate gives you to call; I'm talking about finding people who have managed and reported to this person in the past. LinkedIn is a great platform to find these people. I like to ask the back-channel references questions like, "What is the candidate's biggest blind spots? Would you work with this person again? Is this person a culture keeper or a cultural threat? How does this person deal with conflict? Was this person respected in XYZ company?" My favorite question that I always ask at the end of the call is "one out of ten how would you rate this person?" If it's anything less than a ten, ask why they didn't score them a perfect ten. You will typically more about a candidate by talking to people who worked with them in the past than you will ever learn during an interview.

There are plenty of answers to the question: What makes a leader? But, for me, it's this: Leaders are people who, when they encounter a problem, adversity, or a barrier, work diligently, and try to find a way to overcome it. They have a strong bias towards action and often don't need a lot of guidance; they are doers. Leaders talk about and execute ideas. They do this alone or collectively, with a 'whatever it takes' it takes attitude. They see a problem and look for a new solution. When they fail, they care more about learning from the experience than self-identifying with it. And when their team fails, they are quick to take the blame for the mistake. Conversely, when they win, they always look to give the credit to others. They look toward the future and no matter what has transpired, they always want to move forward, even if the path ahead of them is unclear. They also have humility, treat their team with the ultimate respect and never feel the need to be the "smartest person in the room."

However, a victim is a person who, when they encounter adversity, a setback, or an obstacle, is programmed to point the finger and say, "It's not my fault." It's always someone else's fault. In football, I encountered it in the locker room from a constantly negative player saying things like, "Our coach is a moron," "The offensive coordinator doesn't know what he's doing," or "Our game plans suck." In business, victims feed on office politics, take a defeatist attitude and follow the crowd—even if that crowd is not heading in a positive direction. Victims do not look for new ideas and will criticize without offering a better solution. Don't be a victim.

You may be wondering how this relates to the art of recalibration. It's fairly simple: If you have not embraced setbacks in a positive manner, learned from it, and reprogrammed your compass that leads your towards your goal, it is much harder to become a successful leader. If one views setbacks as a personal failure, or clings to them, one is more likely to emerge as a victim and use blame to shield themselves from admitting a mistake. Any time we're hiring at Integrate, we want to know what happened at his or her previous company. If the person lost their job, why did the company let them go? We know that teams are downsized all the time, but we want to hear how the person perceived the experience. For example, sometimes people go on and on and on about "The company had no idea what they were doing" . . . "My boss was terrible" . . . "The company will never make it" . . . etc. This is a very bad sign, and you want to work alongside people who have enough humility and emotional intelligence to handle these types of situations with more social couth.

Granted, in many cases they may be simply stating a fact, but in my opinion a good leader would describe the situation much differently by saying things like, "The organizational design didn't fit with the type of company I want to work for" or "It never felt like we could lock arms and build a unified culture" or "The values of the company were in conflict with what I believe to be true north."

Anyone Can Stop Being a Victim

What if you realize that perhaps it's *you* who behaves as a victim? That's okay because we have all been a victim in our lives. So how can we get better? Take ownership. Don't be afraid to say, "Yes, I screwed up; that ones on me... my fault, I'll make sure it doesn't happen again." And if you work in an organization or with people who don't understand and respect the fact that everyone makes a mistake, you might want to consider finding another place to take your talents.

Many people fall into patterns of blaming others. If you recognize the pattern, you can then start to work on it. I remember falling into the victim mentality early in my skiing career. I felt like I was skiing better than my competitors and blamed the internal politics of the U.S. Ski Team as the reason I was not allocated more World Cup starts. From the time I was 15 until I was almost 18, I sat stagnant on the U.S. team, and I couldn't stand it.

That frustration drove me to train even harder than I ever thought possible, but because I still believed it was them and not me, mentally I was conditioning myself to think like a victim. What I learned later is that there is only really one cure for internal politics: winning. I learned to use my frustrations as motivation, but to not allow them to shape my thinking. I learned not to slip into the mindset of blaming others for my lack of progress.

Of course, it's often easier to see such patterns in other people than in ourselves. One of the most common types of victims we see all the time is the person who is always late but has an excuse . . . it was the traffic, the phone rang, the elevator was too slow, and on and on. It's a classic victim mentality. They never stop to think that perhaps they must find a solution and plan accordingly to be on time. My parents taught my brother, sister, and me at a young age that honesty was the only policy that would work with them. Their rule was that no matter what we did or how bad we screwed up, if we were honest with them, we would never get in trouble.

If you identify someone as a victim, you should consider sitting them down and talking to him or her. Share with them how you experienced the situation and make sure you come from a place of caring for the other person, not from a place of anger. We aren't born leaders or victims. A victim with the right internal motivation, who is given constructive feedback, can certainly mature into a leader.

Despite trying to weed out the victims, sometimes you will end up with someone who has the "victim mentality" on your team. Perhaps they have mastered the art of interviewing well or even start off with a very positive, nonvictim approach. Their true colors, however, will always surface when something goes wrong, and they blame everyone else for the miscue or mistake. If this becomes a regular response and they don't show improvement after you have given them feedback, you should cut ties quickly, regardless of how great the person is at their job. As an owner, CEO, or leader, you can't let the victim mentality infect your organization because it is highly contagious.

One of my favorite stories of taking a proactive stance, rather than being a victim, occurred shortly after I started Integrate. In our first year, I hired a remote-working employee to do sales in Maryland. His name is Jeremy Dempsey. After about five months on the job, I could see that it was not working out. At that time, I did most of the hiring and the firing. So I called him, thanked him for his efforts, and let him know that I had decided to go in a different direction. I added that I'd be happy to write him a great letter of recommendation.

From Victim To Leader

An incredible story of moving from being a victim to becoming a leader comes from Candy Lightner. When her 13-year-old daughter Laura was killed by a drunk driver, Lightner could have remained a victim, wallowing in the pain and blaming the world for her tragic loss. Instead, she took the position of a leader, forming Mothers Against Drink Driving (MADD), a nationally recognized organization that has had a significant impact on lowering the number of drunk-driving fatalities in America through education and legislation.

There was silence on the other end that seemed to last for an eternity. Then he said, "Oh, really," which usually doesn't mean things are going to go well. Dempsey continued with a suggestion, "How about this. You can take away my base salary and all my commissions, but I'm not leaving. I believe in this company, and I have no doubt in my mind that I am going to crush it here." I was floored by his response. I remember thinking to myself, "This is the type of leader that I would go to war with." We worked out the particulars to keep him onboard. Jeremy went on to be the number one revenue producing sales executive in the business for four consecutive years. Believing in yourself is a known but underutilized skill and Jeremy exemplifies it.

I've told that story to CEOs with 30 years of experience, and none of them had ever heard of something like that. Jeremy refused to be a victim and was out to prove me wrong—and prove himself right.

CHAPTER EIGHT
BUILDING A LOCKED-ARMS CULTURE

As co-founder of Integrate, I was initially inexperienced in the business world and therefore followed the lead of my co-founder in establishing the company culture. However, the culture he created was one of secrecy, where many important matters, including investments, employee ownership stakes, and company performance, were not openly discussed. This lack of transparency caused tension between us and left employees feeling disconnected from the company they worked for. Upon being promoted to CEO by the board of directors, one of my top priorities was to shift the culture towards one of transparency. We strive to provide our employees with open and honest communication about all aspects of the company, including financials, stock options, board decks, and sales.

I learned from my experiences with NFL franchises the impact that culture can have on an organization and believe that fostering a strong business culture is essential for the success and happiness of our employees.

Building a strong culture within a team is at the core of success. I believe that you want a culture that recognizes and embraces shared values, attitudes, standards, and beliefs that characterize the goals of the organization. And it's a good idea to make sure it suits the best people who work at the company while making a positive impression on customers and anyone else associated with the business.

The idea of a top down, stuffy corporate culture was blown up by the tech boom when leaders recognized, and began to quantify, how a strong work-life integration resulted in a better bottom line. Happier, fulfilled, engaged employees were simply more productive than uninformed teammates who were beholden to archaic ideals. Ping-pong tables started popping up in the lobbies of startups; collegial cafes and break rooms replaced cold, bring-your-own-lunch rooms, and as a result, businesses like Google, Facebook, and YouTube broke down the barriers between management and employees. Everyone locked arms.

These modern-day cultures and their values, with fewer boundaries, are a far cry from those of previous generations. Veteran entrepreneur, NYU Stern School of Business professor, and founder of CultureIQ Greg Besner points to the generational shift that is changing the perception of business and has brought culture to the foreground. "Our grandparents' generation of workers had such different career aspirations from today's generation. In the wake of bread lines and world wars, finding a career with long-term stability and fair income was a high priority," Besner says. "But today, the youngest of some 78 million baby boomers are turning 50, and the oldest baby boomers are retiring."

In contrast, the new generation of some 80 million Millennials, those born in the 1980s and 1990s, now entering into leadership positions, has grown up during times of economic growth and tremendous technological advancement. Rather than looking for a job that might someday become a career, they are, as Besner puts it, "placing great significance on the qualitative elements of their career, such as a positive company culture." Rather than retiring with a gold watch after 25 years of service, this generation will have likely changed jobs once if not twice during the first 25 months of employment. Reed Hastings, CEO of Netflix, told me that he doesn't even recognize tenure at the company. Instead, he lionizes performance. Period.

A recent report published by Gallup, called "The State of the American Workplace," identified that 70 percent of American workers are disengaged at work, many business owners took notice and some recognized that they needed to pay closer attention to their company culture if they wanted to stay competitive during this demographic shift in the workplace.

Results of the new cultural awakening in recent years can be seen by the Great Place to Work Institute's annual list of the 100 best companies to work for. The list is topped by companies such as Google, NetApp, Microsoft, and Kimberly

Clark, all of which feature very low turnover, high employee growth and job satisfaction, as well as some amazing revenues. In his book *The Cultural Cycle*, Professor James L. Heskett notes that an "effective culture can account for 20 to 30 percent of the differential in corporate performance when compared with 'culturally unremarkable' competitors."

> *"Culture is like a hairstyle: Everyone has one, even if they're bald. You can either pursue a style that accurately reflects your personality, or you can pretend it doesn't matter and end up looking like Edward Scissorhands."*
> —Drew McLellan, Head of Agency Management Institute

Creating a Culture That Works

Most of the best business cultures are not created haphazardly or spontaneously, but rather result from the efforts of executive teams who understand that leadership involves bringing together the diverse talents, ideas, and abilities of an entire team. As I learned during my time with the Pittsburgh Steelers, Head Coach Mike Tomlin's brand of team culture fostered a sense of unity and collaboration. Establishing a culture that reflects your values means having a clear and consistent vision, as well as a clear understanding of how you want the company to be perceived by both internal and external stakeholders. In the past, many traditional CEOs and leaders prioritized business operations over people, but it is the people who ultimately make a business successful. As such, the greater inclusion of people in the operation of a business often leads to greater contributions from employees, which can translate to increased appreciation from customers. Ultimately, unless you are solely reliant on technology, your business relies on people to produce products and provide services for other people.

The assumption that people should come first seems obvious. With that in mind, in all my efforts to create a team of leaders and not victims, I wanted to integrate into a culture in which we had transparency, one in which everyone in our company knew what was always going on, for better and for worse. I never felt the need to provide only good news and shield people from bad news. In fact, the only way to maximize the talents of your team is to ask for their help in solving problems. When leaders don't share big gaps in the organization they are left to figure out and solve the problems themselves. This is not scalable.

It's a good idea to start by asking your team what values they appreciate most inside an organization. Inviting all your team to contribute to what the ultimate company culture values are will create a better-connected sense of ownership to those values and ensure that one single person isn't speaking for the entire organization.

I first met Tony Bates at a United States Olympic Team fundraising event at the Yellowstone Club in Montana. Tony took over as GoPro's president in 2014 and is seen as one of the best culture builders there is. His advice to me is that I need to relate vision to pragmatic steps. "I think a strategy along with a vision cannot be understated," explains Tony. "Vision can be ambiguous, so having your vision linked to a strategy is very important. When I am coaching the team, I draw this on the board so they can see the need to shape their vision to where they want to go."

Personally, I also believe that it is okay to reach out a little bit beyond everyone's comfort zone when setting up a culture. I think it's good to feel a little bit uncomfortable—it's a sign we're all doing the right thing. For example, it's not traditional to share as much about our financials as we do with our employees. Admittedly, it can feel a bit uncomfortable, but in the end, I would rather retain an employee who wants to work harder to solve problems than one who runs away from them.

Bates adds that in a good culture, it's important to take calculated risks and allow people to enjoy some latitude rather than holding them back. "Before going to Cisco, I worked for a large service provider where I was getting ready to do my first big pitch to executives and was told what I could and couldn't say," says Tony. "I was scared to begin with, and it was so debilitating. I vowed never to work in a culture like that again, and even left the company."

"On the flip side, if a leader does want to have a high-performance organization and a strong culture, they will recognize that it is a collaborative effort," says CultureIQ's Greg Besner, adding that building a culture can include participation by employees in committees and clubs within the overall office culture. He also adds that collecting feedback from employees on engagement surveys, and then communicating that feedback on the areas the company needs to address, helps promote a culture that focuses not only on financial results, but also one that recognizes the significance of nonfinancial results.

Cultural Cornerstones

There is no one-size-fits-all company culture. It will vary depending on several factors, including the type of business, size of the company, background of the founders and management team, and even the design of your facility. Following are some of the things I believe to be the cornerstones of a solid business culture.

Transparency

By now you should know how much I believe in transparency. At Integrate, we go over all key metrics of the business with the entire company. The goal is for all employees to feel they know the thinking, responsibilities, and strategy at various levels of the company and can share ideas and feedback no matter who they are.

Time to Disconnect

I really believe, as do Eric Roza of Datalogix and Brad Feld of the Foundry Group, that people need time off. We all need to hit the reset button occasionally. People cannot come in early and leave late every single day without getting burnt out at some level. While you want employees to have a work-hard founder's mentality, you need to recognize the work-life integration that exists and how significant it is to make sure you have personally fulfilled, clear-thinking people.

Being Good Stewards Of The Data

If you subscribe to the notion of transparency by default, you will want to be clear with your employees that with transparency comes the responsibility of being good stewards of the data. Confidential data must remain in-house and is not for public consumption. With transparency comes a need for mutual trust. There are no exceptions, and transition of the information past company walls is a firing offense.

I know how important time off is for me. It allows everyone to recharge and hit the refresh button. We have unlimited vacation days at Integrate, as do many other startups. Some people view this policy as irresponsible because they have a lack of trust in their team's ability to manage their vacation time. However, I'm a deep believer in managing a business and a team to outcomes rather than outputs. Where an employee lives, how they spend their days, when they take vacation are all outputs. Outcomes are how are they performing, are they hitting their objectives? How is their culture, are they helping others, being collaborative, being a good teammate. These outcomes are much more important to focus on, rather than the outputs.

Take A Needed Break

Tony Schwartz, CEO of The Energy Project and author of *Be Excellent at Anything*, wrote in a 2013 *New York Times* article, "Daytime workouts, short afternoon naps, longer sleep hours, more time away from the office, and longer, more frequent vacations boosts productivity, job performance, and, of course, health." Schwartz backed up his words with research, including a Harvard study which estimated that sleep deprivation costs American companies $63.2 billion a year in lost productivity.

In another study from Oxford Economics, it was noted that Americans, collectively, left roughly 429 million unused paid days off on the table in 2013. "Leaving earned days on the table harms, not helps, employers by creating a less productive and less loyal employee," says Adam Sacks, president of the Tourism Economics division of Oxford Economics.

We also use the OKR management system to quantitatively measure our progress every quarter. OKR stands for Objectives and Key Results, a concept that was built inside of Intel and later put into practice at Google by John Doerr, one of Google's early investors. OKRs, or Key Performance Indicators (KPI), as other companies call them, help your company structure its goal setting. It starts by setting up an objective that is ambitious and broad, something like "build world-class product." How would you measure that? That's where the key results come in. Two key results for that objective could be to successfully implement a QA process and a new product rollout protocol.

By using OKRs, we have quarterly, measurable goals. We keep everyone's OKRs on our internal online network, and we print a quarterly playbook that includes OKRs of the company and each employee. This way, we can all see what went well and what did not. One of the most important aspects of the OKRs is that they are not used as performance tools or for the purposes of evaluations or promotions. They are used as a learning tool to help us determine where we succeeded at reaching our goals, where we fell down, and what we learned from each experience. People know what I am working on, what our CFO is working on, what their officemate is working on, and so on. There are no secrets around our main focus and objectives from the CEO to office assistants. By looking at their own OKRs and those of others, employees can measure personal and group progress and, as John Doerr puts it, stay "in step with each other." That, in turn, creates better communication; everyone knows where each person is in the process.

Informed employees are more involved and empowered in a company. And the more freedom people must take on tasks, manage them, find solutions, and execute them, the more they feel connected to and woven into the company's culture.

Physical Space

Even in this post pandemic world where a lot of us still aren't going into and office, if you haven't watched Susan Cane's TED Talk on introverts, I highly recommend it. She opened my mind to the idea that American businesses are built for extroverts, down to the floor plans of our office spaces. This inspired me to get to know my employees better because although open spaces are great for some, other people need to be able to close the door to be at their most productive. We have several offices with a variety of floor plans. For example, in Boston our space has inner offices where anyone can shut the door if they want to do so. In Boulder, Arizona, Boston, India, and the UK we have designed our spaces around both the needs of introverts and extroverts.

Talking to Customers and Employees

At different points in a company's maturation process, you are almost guaranteed to go through weeks or even months where you feel lost. Organizations deal with these periods in many different ways. Some hold closed-door working sessions to try to solve the problem, inviting only top management. Other companies open up communication and ask for broader input.

Know What Matters Most

As your culture grows, it's a good idea to familiarize yourself with what matters the most to the people with whom you work.

A survey conducted by public relations firm Burson-Marsteller, in conjunction with the Great Place to Work Institute, of senior executives from top-ranked companies in the global workplace ratings yielded the following results:

Companies with the highest ratings:

- Invested more time in their employees, including work-life programs, flex time, health benefits, and perks;
- Are upgrading, offering more programs with stability and career development opportunities.
- Recognize that culture is critical to talent retention.

One way we try to solve problems at Integrate is by talking to our customers. It's a concept that was instilled in me by David Karnstedt, who I talked about in Chapter 6.

When you haven't nailed a product market fit or you're having challenges relating to your product or corporate vision, the natural tendency is to look inside the company and turn your attention to where you or your team went wrong. You might talk to your VP of product, to the CFO, your board of directors, or your sales team. However, over the past four years, whenever we've been stuck at Integrate, I always come back to that one key principle that David taught me: Go talk to your customers.

"I go out to talk to customers because a) you want to understand what works and what doesn't work in the product; b) it helps you refine your approach and know how you are going to market it; and c) probably the most important thing is it fires you up. You get a lot of enthusiasm from being out there with customers and talking to people about your product," David told me.

Today, part of our culture at Integrate is to find out what our customers think, and need, and then work to meet their needs. It sounds fairly obvious, but it is surprising how easy it can be to forget that, especially when you feel stuck.

"I find that as a CEO, or as an executive, it's easy to get so wrapped up in the minutia and the day-to-day operations that you are not out on the front lines as a leader," says David. "So many leaders that I know never go out and talk to their employees without an agenda. I used to schedule time just to walk the halls and get a pulse on how the culture is doing, how the employees are doing, and build and develop relationships. It's much different than a quarterly all-hands meeting, which is not the same as talking to someone and asking how it's going. Making personal connections makes such a difference."

I couldn't agree more. It's one of the reasons why you, as an entrepreneur, executive, or CEO, enjoy coming to work every day.

Optimism Delusion

If you're a person who tends to see the glass half full, it can be easy to fall into something called the optimism delusion—and for leaders, it doesn't always work for the long haul. In fact, it can also cause a breakdown in culture. The idea is that there is a pressure to only share the good news with your team because by sharing the bad news it will kill the company's morale. You try to present a picture that "everything is terrific" while sweeping bad news under the rug. In reality, I believe this is the exact opposite of the right way to build a strong, healthy, solid culture.

By standing up and saying, "Hey, we're getting our butts kicked by XYZ company," or "Hey, we just lost a client because this area of the product is not working," we are being honest and bringing everyone into the real environment to help solve the problem. Be candid and let people know that if, as a team, we don't resolve the issues, there are going to be major problems.

These types of conversations are healthy to have because they build trust, and you will find out very quickly who your best teammates are. If you keep presenting everything as positive, and sweeping everything negative under the rug, eventually the rug becomes a hill and people will start falling off the rug or looking underneath it only to discover that things are not as good as they seem.

Don't Demotivate Your Employees

There are four ways to totally demotivate your employees. The "don't do this" list:

1. *Publicly criticize.* I learned this one the hard way. In sports, it is normal to be criticized in front of your peers when you drop a pass or throw an interception. However, I tried it once in business and the employee quit two weeks later. Criticism is best served in a one-to-one environment by using the "chiropractic method." Massage first with some positive feedback and then crack and realign with the constructive feedback. Praise in public, criticize in private – a good rule of thumb to live by.

2. *Neglect spending one-on-one time with your team.* HR studies show that managers who don't spend time individually with their team members are much more likely to lose an employee.

3. *Fail to provide praise.* When someone does a great job, they want to know that people see it. If they don't, the employee will wonder why they are working so hard. But when giving praise, make it specific so it does not sound patronizing.

4. *Use fear-based motivation.* This can make an employee think more about their job security than doing their actual job.

In the end, whether it's 48 hours, ten seconds, or whether you are by yourself or working with a team, the major keys to success are being able to:

- Accept your new reality
- Set a deadline for the emotional acceptance stage
- Extract what you have learned
- Move on

Hiring to Match Your Culture

Laszlo Bock, who formally ran the people organization at Google, believes in hiring emergent leaders who can step up at the right time and also step back when necessary. They are the ones that fight feverishly when they feel strongly about something but also possess enough humility to acknowledge that they were wrong when presented new supporting facts. Greg Besner, while recognizing that there is sometimes a need for highly trained, experienced specialists in some areas, also says that he favors hiring "great people over great resumes and great experience." Personally, I would never hire someone that I believed to be a culture risk, regardless of his or her competency.

Chad Hurley, co-founder of YouTube, introduced me to Bill Maris in 2009 at TEDMED. Bill was the president and managing director of Google Ventures and was responsible for all of Google's venture investing. Bill and I bonded over our mutual passion for taking better care of the oldest people living in our world today.

Bill, who played a leading role in Google Ventures' 250-plus investments, says that he selects where to put the investment dollars based largely on the person behind the business, even more significantly than their experience or the specific businesses they're trying to launch.

These ideas all make good sense to me, and I have tried to drill them down into the DNA at Integrate. The right people are keys to any organization, and it's not simply about their resume. As I discussed in the previous chapter, your hiring decisions are among the most important decisions you will make. In this chapter, I shed some light on attributes I think are important for the sake of the culture.

Along with emergent leadership, humility and respect are also part of being on a team. People should inherently care about those with whom they work. This is true at all levels from top management to interns. If people have an unhealthy amount of disrespect for one another, the likelihood that the entire organization will have a difficult time achieving a desirable culture will increase. In addition, you also want to have people who have some positive sense of the founder's mentality or ownership.

Get A Pulse On Your Culture

The world is becoming a smaller place, and when you look around the office, you'll likely see people of various ages, from all socioeconomic backgrounds and from all parts of the world," says Greg Besner of CultureIQ. "That's what makes it so important that the communication, the collaboration, the support network, and the workplace environment all tie together as part of your culture. It is part of the reason culture has become such a topic of interest for so many businesses and business leaders."

Over the past couple of years, Besner and his team have focused on developing software to help companies build and monitor the business culture within their office. Using a series of anonymous surveys administered by CultureIQ, feedback from employees is collected and measured. The results can be used to help strengthen a business's existing culture. Data is quantified and the software provides a dashboard for the company to see the metrics, comments, and trends, as well as review nine categories and associated qualities common to high-performance organizations. They are:

- Ownership
- Agility
- Support
- Mission and Value Alignment
- Innovation
- Environment
- Performance Orientation
- Collaboration and Communication
- Wellness

By understanding how your company is performing in these areas, you can evaluate your business culture and see where improvements can be made. The company also offers a library of programs to explore and implement as you try to strengthen company culture.

As a business owner, CEO, or manager, you want to find out how the culture you've created is working. Through research, surveys, and even one-one conversations, you want to be able to answer questions such as:

Do people in your office come to work just for the paycheck or do they really believe in the vision, the products, and the goals of the business?

Do they understand, and care about, the daily pain and challenges the business faces?

Do they understand, and care about, the pain and challenges the customer faces?

Are they active in improving the culture and offer ideas and feedback?

While team members typically do not have the same stake in the business as the managers, owners, or shareholders, they should have a sense that this is their company too and not just a place to spend eight or nine hours a day.

The final quality employees should have, as mentioned in the previous chapter, is competency. While I consider emerging leadership, humility, and a sense of ownership (or founder's mentality) to be more significant for creating the right culture, you still need people who know what they are doing. This does not necessarily come from someone's GPA or resume. It comes from his or her background and from what they have learned along the way.

CHAPTER NINE
THE ROLLER COASTER RIDE

One month before NFL training camp, I was returning a kickoff at the end of practice when I felt a pop in my hamstring. I collapsed to the ground, immediately knowing that something was wrong. I limped off the field and into the training room, where an MRI revealed a two-centimeter tear in my semimembranosus muscle at the top of my hamstring. The doctor told me that I didn't need surgery and if I took a week off, I should be good to go. However, the first time I sprinted again, about a week later, I felt the muscle tear again.

The challenge of a hamstring injury for a sprinter is that you never know when it's fully healed. This was the first time in my athletic career that I had to deal with being sidelined by an injury, and it was a mentally challenging experience. Not only was I unable to play, but I also faced pressure from the team, team physician, and coaches to get back on the field as soon as possible. There's even a saying in the NFL: "You can't make the club in the tub." It took nearly six months for my hamstring to be strong enough for me to sprint again.

Managing our psychology through the ups and downs of life is one of its greatest challenges, whether it be in sports, business, or personal life. The roller coaster of success and failure is something we all must navigate, and it can be especially difficult to handle when we face unexpected setbacks or injuries.

Taking a Ride

There have been numerous instances in my life where I have had to learn to better manage my own psychology, not just when I was injured in the NFL.

As a startup founder, it is common to wake up feeling confident in your product, team, and business, convinced that you will change the world. However, later in the day, you may receive phone calls that reveal you are about to lose a major client or that your servers have completely crashed, and you are unable to conduct any business. Suddenly, the roller coaster plummets, and you begin to wonder how much longer your company will survive. One moment you are riding high, and the next you are at the bottom, looking up.

In the business world, it rarely feels like smooth sailing, and there are plenty of drops along the way. Because of this, I have a constant, nagging feeling that no matter how well we are doing, something can, and likely will, go wrong. Some people call it productive paranoia. It is an uneasy feeling in the back of your mind, but it is productive because it drives you to work harder, pay closer attention, and ensure that you are always checking for potential issues or looking closely at details.

We are a data-driven company that focuses on signs and signals, and we try to determine what is working, what isn't, and where we want to do business. We take risks, but not without thorough research. We identify gaps in our business and try to determine how to fill them. This paranoia leads to heightened awareness and productivity.

The Downward Turn

Our company, Integrate, experienced a near-catastrophic financial crisis early on in our journey. One month, we received a call from our lender informing us that we had broken a loan covenant and, if it chose to do so, the bank could demand that we repay the entire $7 million working cash flow loan immediately. To compound the issue, we had unknowingly broken the covenant, which rarely occurs. It became evident that we had not implemented the necessary financial controls.

As a result, we were on the verge of bankruptcy due to an upcoming payroll and insufficient funds in the bank. I quickly flew to Denver from San Francisco to meet with the bank, using the threat of shutting down the business and incurring losses for all parties as leverage to negotiate a modification of the borrowing base and a $2 million bridge loan until we were able to close a new equity round. Despite some tension, the tactic was successful, and the bank extended the bridge loan and forgave the broken covenant. We were also able to raise an additional $6 million from our existing investors.

While the resolution was welcomed, it did not go without consequences. I will never forget being reprimanded by the Comcast partnership, specifically by Amy Banse, the former Managing Director at Comcast Ventures. It is crucial for entrepreneurs to understand the importance of hiring competent financial leaders from the outset of the business. Our failure to do so nearly caused the collapse of Integrate."

Another company that faced the brink of bankruptcy and was able to turn things around was US Airways. In 2003, the airline industry was facing a crisis due to rising fuel prices and increased competition from low-cost carriers. US Airways was struggling to stay afloat with over $11 billion in debt and dwindling revenues. The company filed for Chapter 11 bankruptcy protection and implemented a restructuring plan that included cutting over 6,000 jobs and grounding over 100 planes.

However, the company's leadership team, led by CEO Doug Parker, didn't give up on the airline's future. They worked to negotiate better deals with suppliers and labor unions, and eventually merged with America West Airlines in 2005 to create a larger and more competitive carrier.

Over the next decade, US Airways continued to focus on cost-cutting measures and expanding its route network. In 2013, the company merged with American Airlines to create the world's largest airline, and the combined company is now known as American Airlines Group.

Despite facing bankruptcy and numerous challenges, US Airways was able to turn things around and ultimately achieve success through strong leadership, strategic decision-making, and a focus on efficiency and cost-cutting.

When the Bubble Bursts

Prior to his position as the CEO of Skype or his current role as CEO of Genesys, Tony Bates learned the ups and downs of business during the dotcom boom of the late 1990s and the subsequent crash of 2001. "It was early on in my tenure at Cisco Systems . . . we were having the time of our life with the boom of the internet, and I was working on the high-end router products," says Tony. "Obviously, when the bubble burst, it had a big impact on Cisco and made us realize how quickly things could change. It was a major learning experience for me. We had reached a point where we were actually the number-one largest market cap company for one day. Exxon was number two. What's interesting is that when you're in the middle of something like that, it's very hard to recognize that it's a bubble that can burst. "I believed everything they were saying about the dotcom industry because I was part of it and part of helping to build it.

I remember being at a leadership conference and people were talking about how we could go to a trillion dollars in market cap! I remember walking out of that leadership conference and saying, 'Okay, I'm in and already to go.' Then, when it all went crazy, I remember asking myself, 'How did I really buy into that when it made no sense?' "It was a significant lesson for me, learning to become more objective and much more long term in my thinking, rather than getting caught up in the short term—it's really an important perspective. Often the way people learn is by experiencing a big shock in some way. That taught me a lot about leadership. That was the first time I experienced such a crash, and I had to make tough budget decisions, the kind that test your leadership capabilities on a human and strategic level. "I guess I passed the test but knew that I never want to be caught in such a situation again."

Not unlike failing, such a plunge can also provide some excellent lessons. While I can't say I'm glad it happened, I will say that it did provide me with much greater insights into the financial end of the business, and I have since been much more aware of where we stand financially.

Managing Risk

Every business endeavor involves taking a risk. When you open your doors or launch your website, you are taking a risk that there might not be a sufficient market for your product, that it might be too costly or difficult to reach your target audience, or that a competitor may beat you to the punch. To mitigate these risks, it is essential to conduct thorough research, testing, and consultation with key stakeholders, particularly your customers. It is also crucial to keep a close eye on your industry and stay aware of your competitors' actions. As CEO, I made a promise to myself to minimize unnecessary risks and to mature our business from a more impulsive approach to one that leverages data to make more informed, calculated decisions. In times of adverse news, one of my board members and mentors, Seth Levine, always advises:

1. Don't panic.
2. Gather information.
3. Make an informed decision.

It can be tempting to react impulsively to negative news, but it is much more effective to take a step back, assess the information objectively, and devise a plan of action.

Tuning Out the Noise

I talked about drowning out the noise when discussing intrinsic versus extrinsic motivation. It's also imperative when trying to focus on the path ahead of you in business. Having survived the whirlwind of negativity surrounding the bursting of the dotcom bubble while at Cisco, Tony Bates now handles the ups and downs of the internet world without great anxiety.

"It helped me put it all into perspective," he says. "At Skype, people would read about what others were saying and say, 'We've already won, we've destroyed the telecommunication industry,' which, first of all, wasn't true, we only disrupted it. Secondly, I reminded people that it's just one of many innings and that great companies are always in marathons, they're not in sprints."

Tony believes you should have filters in place for much of the reporting you read and hear. "Tuning out the noise is a good strategy but hard to implement in reality," Tony told me, adding that it's important to make a list of the right people to pay attention to. This would include:

1. Customers
2. Employees
3. Shareholders

"All of the others you try to block out," Tony advises.

But, he says, it's also something to remember when you have to filter your own message. "One of my lowest moments was when I was at Skype and we made some management changes," Tony recalls. "There was a headline that basically said that we let them go because we didn't want to pay them out. Of course, this got a lot of press and a lot of emotional responses in the Valley. It was a complicated situation, but what I didn't realize was that I didn't do enough to get the full story out there, to explain what was really happening. If I had it to do over, I would have handled it much differently and explained the situation in greater detail." For entrepreneurs, getting their own message out early and often is crucial.

Finding a Balance

Maintaining emotional neutrality during times of stress and success is a crucial skill for managing the inevitable ups and downs of life, business, and athletics. People who possess this ability, such as New England Patriots coach Bill Belichick and San Antonio Spurs coach Gregg Popovich, are able to stay even keeled and maintain a level head in all situations. Cultivating this ability requires training and discipline, but it ultimately allows for better decision-making and resilience in the face of challenges.

Let Endorphins Help You

To maintain a healthy mindset and balance in the face of the constant ups and downs of business and life, I have found that consistent exercise is a key component. When you engage in physical activity, your body releases endorphins, which are chemicals that help to reduce stress and improve your overall mood. This can lead to a sense of euphoria and increased energy, helping you to better handle the challenges and setbacks that inevitably arise. It's important to make exercise a regular part of your routine, rather than just turning to it in times of stress, to sustain a positive outlook and build resilience in the face of adversity.

If it's something you struggle with, know that balancing starts with an understanding of why it is important to stay emotionally even. As I see it, the higher you are, the further you can fall, and that cycle of riding the emotional roller coaster and getting yourself up when you're down, and then going back down, is exhausting. As a result, you expend too much energy and too much time overthinking the situation. This energy could be put to better use elsewhere.

The way each person achieves narrowing the emotional gap and trying to be more even is largely dependent on each person's personality.

When I was with the Steelers, Coach Tomlin constantly told us that he wanted a boring football team. "I want us to pack our lunch pails, get our work done, and go home without any of the flash. I want a boring-ass football team," he would say.

I didn't fully understand it then, but I think the sense of "boring" that Tomlin meant was the idea of being steadier and more predictable. If you rein in the emotions and remain somewhat consistent every day, you may be a little more boring, but you will be predictable—and predictability works very well in business.

Companies working with predictable leadership have more consistency, and this also spills over outside of the organization where customers will know what to expect and what they can count on from your business.

In the End, It's All Worthwhile

You've probably seen kids, and adults for that matter, who are apprehensive waiting in line to ride a roller coaster. They aren't sure what they are in for, and some get onboard rather tentatively. Then, a few minutes later, the ride is over, and they leave smiling, glad they went. Whether they loved it or not, they will say, "I'm glad I had the chance to ride it."

When I asked Apolo Ohno what he thought about the roller coaster ride, he said, "It's been awesome!" He's thankful to have been on board. "When I was 18 or 19 years old, I had the world at my fingertips, but I didn't have anybody to teach me what was coming up after sports." He greatly appreciates that he was fortunate to stay on top of his sport for more than a decade.

"I learned, I made mistakes, and I have certainly been through the roller coaster ride," adds Apolo. "I think if you just have one linear path of uphill progress it's kind of boring. No great athlete in the world has won every race or every title, not even the greatest of the greats . . . Michael Jordan, Michael Johnson, they had their failures. Without failures we don't learn for ourselves. Unfortunately, in business it's not like there's another race coming up. You must put so much into it, money, time, and so on, and you have to make sure you've got your bases covered. I think it's a lot more painful when you fail in a business, but you still must rebound and start up that roller coaster ride all over again, using what you've learned."

He's so right, as evidenced by all the entrepreneurs who have watched one company flounder or fail and the next one, or the one after that, take them up to the top of the mountain once again—or for the first time.

CHAPTER TEN
A RISING TIDE LIFTS ALL BOATS

As I reflected on the world around me, I couldn't help but notice the vast disparities in opportunities and resources available to different individuals. While some people seem to effortlessly achieve their goals and dreams, others struggle to even have their aspirations recognized. This realization motivated me to strive to make a positive impact on at least one other person's life, if not more. This desire to give back and make a difference was instilled in me by my mother, while my father, a highly successful clinical psychologist and talented athlete, served as a constant source of inspiration and guidance for me. He taught me the value of hard work and determination, and consistently pushed me to be my best self. Growing up, he also served as my football and ski coach, and instilled in me a love for sports and competition. Despite his demanding schedule, working six days a week to support our family, he always made time to invest in my personal growth and development. Whenever I face a challenging issue, he is the first person I turn to for wise counsel.

My mom, too, loved and supported my dreams of becoming a successful athlete. She did not miss a single college football game that I played in and would often travel the world to see me ski. However, she always told me, "I'm less concerned if you win a gold medal and care more about how you treat people and what you do to give back to the world." My mom is the ultimate nurturer. I believe that she was put on this world to love and take care of things and people. I am so lucky to have her as my mom. I had two incredible parents who helped shape my life, and they remain two of my best friends, biggest fans, and determined advocates.

I'm proud of what I was able to accomplish in athletics. But there is something more to a legacy, no matter what level of success someone has achieved. You don't have to be an Olympic athlete to have achieved success. The truth is that success comes from making changes in your community, building a thriving small business, raising children you can be proud of, having your novel published, or affording the vacation home you've always wanted.

However, when it comes to a legacy, in my view, it is something that you build for somebody else, not for yourself. While I might inspire young athletes on the slopes or on the field, or young hires at Integrate, it's not the same as specifically doing things for other people.

One of the reasons I started a nonprofit, called Wish of a Lifetime, was because I was guilty of living the professional athlete selfish existence. To succeed as a collegiate or professional athlete, you must do a lot of things that are deeply rooted in being selfish. You must focus on yourself and do whatever it takes to accomplish your goals. It's so competitive that you can't focus elsewhere, and, in large part because of that, you end up being selfish. At the time you don't even realize it because you are so focused on reaching your goal and blocking out the outside world.

A Father's Take: Larry Bloom

Two of the most valuable people in my life I did not have to seek out: my parents.

My dad has been there with me for the whole ride, up and down the mountains, through the agony of sitting on the sidelines with a long hamstring injury in football, and as I ride the roller coaster that is starting a business. Larry Bloom, a clinical psychologist for 40 years, saved me a bundle on therapy costs and has a lot to say about how I got where I am today. I asked him to comment on my journey, through his own eyes.

"Starting at a young age, Jeremy demonstrated a great deal of talent, but along the way, whether it was in skiing, football, or track and field, he also experienced setbacks. Even though he was a high-achievement-oriented kid, he fell, stumbled and experienced a lack of achieving from time to time, as is the case when facing challenges.

"Under the circumstances, he had to learn to deal with it, and he did. You must do so if you're going to get further up the ladder. You must learn to deal with the failures and the realization that you won't always succeed. It's part of sports and part of business.

"There is also a need to know what you can and cannot control. I remember when Jeremy was vying to become one of three or four Americans to make the Olympic team in 2002. He had to go through the arduous process of competing. And no matter how well you do, it's not always clear whom the coaches are going to pick for the team. It's not necessarily objective. He called me from France one evening and said to me, 'Dad, I'm stressed. I don't know what they're going to do or how they're going to handle it.' I remember telling him, 'Jeremy, you are trying to control something you have no control over. You cannot control what the coaches are going to do or what discretionary choices they are going to make; all you have is control over yourself. So, you must push that away, get up tomorrow morning, and forget about what they are going to do . . . just get to the point where you are doing better every single day. That's all you focus on.'

"The other important aspect of Jeremy's careers is that he found people to turn to. It helps to have mentors and relationships with people whom you know well and trust. I would say learning how to deal with failures and setbacks, understanding what you can and cannot control, and building a network of people you can turn to are all important aspects of Jeremy's life that have helped him.

"Business doesn't always go as planned. We've had many conversations in recent years, and I know that getting involved in a startup means you're going to have hills and valleys. He approaches the business, the peaks and valleys and the setbacks, in the same way as he did in sports."

My Inspiration for Helping Seniors

My attention gravitated toward seniors largely because of my grandparents. For most of us, inspiration to give back—in small and large ways—naturally comes from that which is closest to us, such as the people living with us. When I grew up, my mom's mother, Donna, was living downstairs in our home. For the first 19 years of my life, it was my mom, dad, brother, sister, and my grandmother. She was like a second mother to me. Today, she lives in Keystone, Colorado, high in the Rocky Mountains, and at the age of 89 still drives through the snow and ice to volunteer at the elementary school and at local senior center. She has the most wonderful outlook on life, and although she has many challenges, I never hear her complain.

Meanwhile, my dad's father, who passed away in 2014, was one of my best friends growing up. When I was three years old, he was my first ski instructor and would throw miniature-sized candy bars down the mountain to teach me how to ski. A huge Denver Broncos and Miami Dolphins fan, he also helped increase my passion for football.

At 17, I traveled to Asia for the first time for a World Cup skiing competition. I remember one afternoon as I was riding on a crowded bus, through the busy streets of Tokyo, a woman who appeared to be at least 80 years of age got on the bus, and nearly everyone who was seated stood up to politely offer her their seats. Then, as the bus started moving again, they each bowed to her. I was a bit awestruck by the reverence directed toward this elderly woman. Was she famous? No, she was simply being respected as one of their elders.

As I traveled around the world over the next decade, I saw similar acts of respect and kindness to seniors not only throughout Asia, but also in Scandinavian countries and elsewhere. It made me think about our country and how in some ways, we are completely backwards in the way we treat the oldest people in our society. We spend so much of our time focused on the youth, always looking for the up-and-comers, while often turning a cold shoulder to the people who gave us life, shaped our world, and fought wars to defend our freedom.

Starting a Nonprofit

Starting my own nonprofit was never a dream of mine. I turned down the idea of starting the Jeremy Bloom Foundation while I was playing sports because I felt the only reason my agents wanted me to launch it was for PR and marketing purposes. However, there wasn't another nonprofit granting wishes to our country's oldest people on a large scale, so I decided to start Wish of a Lifetime in 2008. It has been the most meaningful journey of my life because the feeling of being a small part in helping a 90-year-old person experience something they have dreamed about their entire life is a feeling of purpose that I had never experienced before in athletics.

I had no idea what I was doing when I started. I was playing with the Steelers in the summer of 2008, and I had some time off prior to the pre-season. I filled out a 30-

page IRS form used to apply for tax-exempt status (501(c)(3) status).

The process after that isn't as daunting as it seems, although it does take some time. Even at a small, community-based level, it's possible to start and run a small nonprofit focused on whatever matters most to you. About six months later, we were approved and could begin accepting tax-free donations. During the approval process I started building a board of directors and created bylaws for the organization. Then I planned a visit to an existing organization that worked with seniors so I could figure out what people at this age wished for. One of my early board members, Laura Wildt, hooked me up with the Volunteers of America charity, which has a program to help senior citizens find children to mentor. It was a good place to start; it gave me the opportunity to meet seniors and get to know them.

It was there that I met a woman named Nancy Tarpin. Nancy had no idea who I was or why I was there, but we struck up a conversation about our families and about growing up in Colorado during different generations. She was a very low-income senior, 86 years old, but still active in her community. And she was very engaging. At one point, I asked her what her one wish in life was, if she could do anything she wanted. She told me that her daughter Lucille lived in Arizona and had been diagnosed with ovarian cancer ten years before. She had not seen her daughter in more than a decade, as she didn't have the money to make the trip. She told me that it tore her heart out to know that she was going to lose her daughter without being able to say goodbye. I was floored. Here I was, traveling around the world as a skier and football player, born into an opportunity-rich family, able to support all my dreams. And there was a sweet woman living one short flight away from a daughter who was fighting for her life, and this woman didn't have the means to spend time with her.

One week later, Nancy and I were on a flight to Arizona. I drove her to Claypool, where we met Lucille at a Denny's. I said hello to Lucille and dropped Nancy off to spend time with her. Three days later I drove back up to Claypool. Nancy was a completely different woman. She was smiling from ear to ear and didn't stop smiling all the way back to Denver. Nancy is normally a very quiet person. But the entire way back to Colorado, I don't think there was a moment of silence. She told me every detail of her trip.

It was such a powerful experience, not only for her but also for me. Truthfully, it was one of the most powerful experiences of my life. In that moment, I had played a small part in changing somebody's life, even for a brief time. It hadn't cost much to do it, either. I had never done something like that before. In the past, all my goals were centered on myself, winning gold medals and football games. At the time I contemplated returning to skiing to compete in my third Olympics in Vancouver, Canada. However, after my experience with Nancy I remember calling my mom and telling her that I had found my new mission in life and that this foundation was going to have a huge impact for so many people. I retired the next week from the U.S. Ski Team, and for the next two years, before I started Integrate, Wish of a Lifetime was my sole focus.

Growing Pains

We started small. I seeded Wish of a Lifetime with $25,000 and hired a part-time executive director, Patrick Sablich, to work with me. We didn't open an office; we worked out of coffee shops to start. The nonprofit was the first chapter in my post-athletic career, and I learned a lot of great lessons. In starting a nonprofit, I mixed up a few steps. And if I were to start another one in the future, there are things I would change.

One of the errors in judgment was that I thought that my name recognition and notoriety would automatically translate into donations and support. My game plan was to build a website, then go on TV to talk about the new cause and play up a fundraiser that I planned to have. And I did just that. I received a lot of nice emails wishing us luck, but not a single ticket was sold. We cancelled the fundraiser.

Talk about Recalibrate . . . I was now more determined than ever to make this happen. The mistake I made was not recognizing that it takes a grassroots effort to build a nonprofit from the ground up. In the beginning stages there is nothing more important than creating a solid board of directors. It's more important than your website and more important than your marketing. You must start by building an operational board, which could be five to fifteen people, depending on the scope of the projects you hope to accomplish. This will be your "staff," and you must be upfront with these people, letting them know that you're going to need their services in various capacities from providing advice to planning events to helping you scale the nonprofit. Whatever they can do, you'll need it, especially networking—that's where the fundraising comes from, I learned.

It's hard to get people to jump onboard, but fortunately I found 12 people, including a financial expert, marketing expert, legal expert, several high-net-worth individuals, and some worker bees who had free time to dedicate to the mission. In a nonprofit, time is a very valuable commodity. As important is making sure that the people you choose are engaged in the mission for similar reasons. Each of my board members was committed to the mission; they had stories to tell about how they too believed that the senior population had done so much for us and still had so much more to give.

Mission And Vision Statement

Wish of a Lifetime (WOL) envisions a world in which society embraces aging and the inherent wisdom that accompanies it, where seniors are celebrated for their accomplishments and sacrifices and where intergenerational connections are part of our daily life.

Our belief is that growing older doesn't mean you have to stop dreaming and living a life of purpose. Most elderly men and women have something in their life that they have always wanted to do or see, but for many different reasons they have not been able to live out these dreams.

By connecting seniors to people, purpose, and passions through the granting of their wishes, WOL is able to relieve the feelings of isolation that many seniors live with. WOL engages the hearts and minds of young and old alike by sharing our Wish Recipients' stories.

A year later, after we had all teamed up to network and let people know about Wish of a Lifetime, we held a fundraiser.

This time I leaned on my board to sell 20 tickets each, so they went out and hit their networks, and with a month left to go, we sold out all 500 tickets!

After a very successful first fundraiser I was able to invest more and hire a few additional people. Once we gained traction locally in Colorado, I wanted to expand nationally without spending a lot of money on staffing, so I partnered with the largest senior living company in the United States, Brookdale Senior Living. But first I had to convince them that it was their social duty to grant wishes to their residents. I reached out to one of their vice presidents, Sara Terry, and requested a meeting. I flew to their Chicago headquarters and gave a two-hour presentation to her and her team. Sara and I hit it off from the very beginning; it felt like she was someone that I had known my whole life. She also believed deeply in our mission, and serendipitously Brookdale's corporate values mirrored our mission almost perfectly. At the end of the meeting we agreed in principle to a multiyear deal that would enable Wish of a Lifetime to expand nationally with a volunteer staff at Brookdale. The company became our founding sponsor and has helped us fund hundreds of wishes.

Some Wishes Granted

In April 2014, *People* magazine ran a short story about a unique reunion of three sisters who had not seen each other in many years. Rose Shloss, a 101-year-old Wish of a Lifetime recipient, was reunited with her older sisters, Ruth Branum, 104, and Rubye Cox, 110. They are the remaining three of seven siblings, living in different parts of the country. The

People magazine story, Facebook post, and video inspired nearly 100,000 "likes" and 20,000 shares. It was the kind of heartwarming story that brought attention to the foundation and inspiration to seniors everywhere.

Another wish: A former member of both the United States Navy and Air Force for ten years each, 84-year-old Dan wanted to return to an active submarine for a visit. He loved life in the submarines where he served as physician examiner and later as a surgeon in the Navy's submarine service.

During the Korean War, Dan traveled on multiple tours of sea duty aboard a submarine rescue vessel as well as in one of 12 submarines that were part of his squadron. The problem with getting Dr. Dan back on a submarine to fulfill his wish of a lifetime was the difficulty in climbing up and down the narrow ladders within the vessel. Dan had a short ladder built to practice climbing up and down until he felt he could handle the task. The staff at the King's Bay Naval Base in Georgia then supplied a special ladder/staircase on the USS Maryland, an active U.S. nuclear submarine, to make Dan's dream of being on a submarine again a reality.

Then there's 93-year-old Warren, of Troy, Ohio, who grew up working on a farm that had been in his family for more than 100 years. It was there that he had harvested corn, hay, and beans to make a living for his family. After Warren and his wife left the farm, they turned it over to their children. Warren wanted to see the farm from a new perspective—he wanted to look down at the land from a hot air balloon. Through the foundation, his wish came true, and he got an aerial view of his family's legacy.

These are the kinds of wishes that come true and make everyone involved with Wish of a Lifetime beam with joy.

Your Own Legacy

"I think at the end of the day what will mark success for me will be what I've been able to do for other people," David Karnstedt says. "If the people you've worked with go off to higher levels of success, then you have had an impact. So I'd like my legacy to be about having influenced people positively in a way that they can go off and be successful at whatever it is they do."

Dying Regrets

In 2013, *The Huffington Post* published the top five regrets of the dying, based on research on the topic.

1. I wish I'd had the courage to live a life true to myself, not the life others expected of me.
   "This was the most common regret of all. When people realize that their life is almost over and look back clearly on it, it is easy to see how many dreams have gone unfulfilled. Most people had not honored even a half of their dreams and had to die knowing that it was due to choices they had made, or not made. Health brings a freedom very few realize, until they no longer have it."

2. I wish I hadn't worked so hard.
   "This came from every male patient that I nursed. They missed their children's youth and their partner's

companionship. Women also spoke of this regret, but as most were from an older generation, many of the female patients had not been breadwinners. All of the men I nursed deeply regretted spending so much of their lives on the treadmill of a work existence."

3. I wish I'd had the courage to express my feelings.
"Many people suppressed their feelings in order to keep peace with others. As a result, they settled for a mediocre existence and never became who they were truly capable of becoming. Many developed illnesses relating to the bitterness and resentment they carried as a result."

4. I wish I had stayed in touch with my friends.
"Often they would not truly realize the full benefits of old friends until their dying weeks and it was not always possible to track them down. Many had become so caught up in their own lives that they had let golden friendships slip by over the years. There were many deep regrets about not giving friendships the time and effort that they deserved. Everyone misses their friends when they are dying."

5. I wish that I had let myself be happier.
"This is a surprisingly common one. Many did not realize until the end that happiness is a choice. They had stayed stuck in old patterns and habits. The so-called 'comfort' of familiarity overflowed into their emotions, as well as their physical lives. Fear of change had them pretending to others, and to themselves, that they were content, when deep within, they longed to laugh properly and have silliness in their life again."

Most often, I've found that legacies do not revolve around the letters people achieve after their names or how much money they made. When I looked at a study of people in hospice care, their greatest regrets were also not about money, but things like not letting themselves be happier more often, not spending enough time with friends, or not having the courage to express their feelings. These were personal thoughts and personal regrets.

Consider how Roger Staubach, who served in Vietnam and commanded 41 enlisted men, won two Super Bowl rings during an outstanding NFL career, and became an enormously successful real estate mogul, answered the question, "How do you want to be remembered?"

"I think the most important thing I'd like people to say about me is that he's been a faithful husband and good father," says Staubach. "I'm so proud to say I have five kids, 15 grandchildren, and one great-grandson. That's at the top of my list, and I feel very blessed. I'm always grateful that I got to play for a great football team and I had a great mentor in Mr. Miller in the real estate business. There are a lot of people that have an effect on your life, and for that I'm thankful, but family is always most important to me."

It's Not Always Good to be King: Building a Legacy

Sometimes an incredible legacy story comes late in life, as is the case for Brian Swette, who spent 17 years at PepsiCo and six years as the chairman of the board at Burger King.

"I tell people that the first 17 years my career was designed around getting people to drink larger and larger quantities of soda, and then I moved on to Burger King," says Swette, who considers his life after 60, as co-founder of Sweet Earth Natural Foods, to be a legacy project.

"My interest in sustainable healthy food came from the pivotal understanding that what I was doing wasn't good for anyone, as well as a maturity about how important a plant-based diet can be both for sustainability and health." Swette cites three factors that eventually changed the course of his life—the words of a departing staffer, his daughter, and a fortuitous invitation.

"At PepsiCo, a longtime employee walked up to me one day and told me he was quitting. It was right out of the blue, and I asked him why. He said three words: 'corn fructose syrup.' This was years ago, and I had no idea what he was talking about, so I asked him to be more specific. He said, 'It's a drug, it's evil, it's really bad, and it's hurting people,' so I started to investigate."

Swette also points to the time his daughter, while in high school and taking tests to get into a good college, told him that she had become a vegetarian. Concerned whether she would get enough protein, he once again investigated.

And finally, there was the Global Institute for Sustainability. "They had invited educators on sustainability along with people from the corporate world, which included me, coming from Burger King. I had little to say but learned a lot," explains Swette.

Roughly six years ago, Swette walked away from Burger King and the corporate world. Together with his wife, a former engineer at PepsiCo and ex-head of marketing at

Calvin Klein, he started Sweet Earth Natural Foods. "It's all about meat-free, plant-based food that tastes good," says Swette, who says that he did everything that you are not supposed to do when starting a business, such as using your own money and entering the low-margin food business.

"I believe that this is a form of redemption," says Swette, adding, "I believe in second chances."

In 2020, we had a meeting with AARP's senior leadership team and collectively decided to join forces to take Wish of a Lifetime to the next level. We now sit inside of AARP leveraging their development team and national staff to further scale our mission to grant wishes across the country. We couldn't be more excited to be working alongside our new partners and have big plans over the next several decades.

I find it fascinating, the legacies that people build and how they want to be remembered. As hard as we strive for money, fame, and prestige in our careers, so many people look at those areas of life that touch other people. Helping other people and also learning from them puts so many aspects of life into proper perspective.

EPILOGUE
THE TRAIL TO PURPOSE

Throughout my career, I have been driven to pursue my passions in football, skiing, and business. While I have achieved many of my goals, I have also faced setbacks and failures. These experiences have taught me valuable lessons about art of recalibration and how to adapt in the face of adversity. Based on these experiences, I have developed a set of principles that I believe are crucial for achieving success.

No matter who you are, how successful you've become, how many trophies you've won, or how much money you have attained, you too will fall short of your expectations at some point in your life.

When you do, I hope that you remember some of the key principles inside the lessons of recalibration. Some of the most important aspects include setting a timeframe to move on, not personalizing the moment, focusing on learnings, and committing yourself to moving forward at 100 mph.

Recalibration is not an easy process, but it is essential to achieve your goals and continue growing as a person. I made a very concerted effort to learn how to motivate myself intrinsically, based on doing the best I could possibly do and not setting out to beat the competition or prove myself to other people.

The transition from external motivation was not easy, but once I lost that need to please others, I accomplished more, and recalibrating became easier. I also learned the importance of planting many seeds and not having all my eggs in one basket. I found passions and investigated to see if they led to the right course for me. I've also tried to surround myself with positive, intelligent people who inspire and challenge me. Having people to talk to and learn from is so valuable.

I've included the thoughts of some of my mentors in the pages of this book. They, and others, have provided me with knowledge and wisdom that has helped me on my journey. We can't accomplish every goal; however, enriching experiences on the journey through life happen somewhere between the dream and reality, even if we fall a few times along the way.

As we move forward, let us remember to dream and to embrace the limitless opportunities that are available to us. And let us strive to be the best versions of ourselves, leaving a legacy of positivity and impact on the world around us.

INCREDIBLE STORIES OF RECALIBRATION

ONE
THE UNSTOPPABLE DRIVE - THE STORY OF WILMA RUDOLPH

Wilma Rudolph was born on June 23, 1940, in Saint Bethlehem, Tennessee, into a family with 21 siblings. As the 20th child, she faced numerous challenges from the very beginning. Born prematurely and weighing only 4.5 pounds, Wilma's early life was marked by illness and adversity, forcing her to recalibrate her goals and perspective time and time again.

At the age of four, Wilma contracted polio, a debilitating disease that left her left leg weak and with limited mobility. Doctors predicted that she would never walk again, but Wilma's mother refused to accept this prognosis. She was determined to help her daughter overcome the odds and lead a normal life. Little did she know that her daughter's journey would become a powerful testament to resilience, recalibration, and the human spirit.

With the unwavering support of her family, Wilma began a rigorous regimen of physical therapy. She and her mother traveled 100 miles round trip every week to the closest hospital that treated Black patients, where she received treatment to improve her leg's strength and mobility. At home, her family members took turns massaging her leg, and Wilma practiced walking with a brace, diligently working to improve her condition.

Despite the challenges she faced, Wilma was driven to excel. Her perseverance and determination led her to not only walk without a brace but to become a gifted athlete. At the age of 12, she was able to remove the brace entirely and began playing basketball. Her remarkable progress was an early indication of her ability to recalibrate her expectations and push herself to achieve greatness, even in the face of adversity.

Wilma's athletic talent caught the attention of Tennessee State University track and field coach Ed Temple, who invited her to join his summer training program. It was there that Wilma discovered her passion for running and her exceptional talent for sprinting. With Coach Temple's guidance, she honed her skills and set her sights on even greater achievements.

Wilma's hard work and recalibration of her abilities led her to incredible success in the world of track and field. At the age of 16, she competed in the 1956 Melbourne Olympics, winning a bronze medal in the 4x100-meter relay. However, it was at the 1960 Rome Olympics that she truly made history and showcased her ability to overcome the most daunting challenges.

ONE

In Rome, Wilma Rudolph became the first American woman to win three gold medals in a single Olympic Games. She won the 100-meter, 200-meter, and 4x100-meter relay events, breaking world records and earning the title of "the fastest woman in the world." Her incredible accomplishments brought her international fame and recognition, making her an icon of perseverance and determination.

Wilma used her newfound platform to inspire others and promote racial integration in the United States. Upon returning from the Rome Olympics, she insisted that her homecoming parade and banquet in Clarksville, Tennessee, be racially integrated events – a first for her hometown. Her actions demonstrated her commitment to breaking down barriers and using her success to create positive change in society.

Throughout her life, Wilma continued to break barriers and use her experiences to inspire others. After retiring from competitive athletics, she completed a bachelor's degree in elementary education at Tennessee State University and began working as a teacher and coach. She understood the power of education and mentorship in shaping the lives of young people and was determined to give back to her community.

In 1981, Wilma established the Wilma Rudolph Foundation, a nonprofit organization dedicated to providing support and training for young athletes. The foundation's mission is to inspire and empower youth to realize their full potential, regardless of the challenges they face. Through sports clinics, educational programs, and mentorship opportunities, the Wilma Rudolph Foundation has had a lasting impact on countless young lives.

Wilma's autobiography, "Wilma," was published in 1977, and it chronicled her incredible journey from childhood illness to Olympic glory. The book offered readers a candid and inspiring look at her life, her struggles, and her unwavering determination to succeed. In 1979, the story was adapted into a television film, further spreading her message of resilience and determination to a wider audience.

Throughout her life, Wilma received numerous accolades for her achievements both on and off the track. She was inducted into the U.S. Olympic Hall of Fame in 1983, and in 1993, she was honored with the National Sports Award for her contributions to American sports. In 1994, she was posthumously inducted into the National Women's Hall of Fame, recognizing her lasting impact as a trailblazer and role model for women in sports.

Wilma Rudolph passed away on November 12, 1994, at the age of 54, but her legacy of recalibration, resilience, and the human spirit continues to inspire generations. Her life serves as a reminder that when we face adversity, we can choose to recalibrate our perspectives and use our challenges to our advantage, transforming our struggles into the fuel that drives us toward greatness.

TWO
THE POWER OF TRANSFORMATION - THE STORY OF BETHANY HAMILTON

Bethany Hamilton was born on February 8, 1990, on the island of Kauai, Hawaii. Raised by a family of avid surfers, Bethany's love for the ocean and surfing was deeply ingrained in her from a young age. Her talent for riding the waves was evident, and it seemed as if she was destined for a career in professional surfing.

On October 31, 2003, at the age of 13, Bethany's life changed forever. While surfing with her best friend and her family off the coast of Kauai, she was attacked by a 14-foot tiger shark. The shark bit off her left arm just below the shoulder, causing her to lose 60% of her blood and leaving her fighting for her life.

Bethany's spirit remained strong even in the face of this life-threatening adversity. Just one month after the attack, she was back in the ocean, learning to surf with one arm. This was the beginning of her incredible journey of recalibration and resilience.

Determined not to let the shark attack define her life, Bethany focused on adapting her surfing technique to compensate for the loss of her arm. She learned to paddle and maintain her balance with one arm, finding new ways to excel in the sport she loved. Her passion and determination fueled her progress, and within two years, she was competing again in national surfing competitions.

Bethany's incredible story of recovery and perseverance captured the hearts of people around the world. She used her newfound platform to inspire others, sharing her story and promoting the importance of shark conservation. In 2004, her autobiography, "Soul Surfer: A True Story of Faith, Family, and Fighting to Get Back on the Board," was published, further spreading her message of resilience and faith.

In 2011, Bethany's story was adapted into a feature film called "Soul Surfer," which showcased her journey of recalibration and the power of overcoming adversity. The film brought her inspiring story to an even wider audience, proving that challenges can be transformed into opportunities for growth and achievement.

Throughout her surfing career, Bethany continued to defy the odds, competing in prestigious events and earning numerous accolades. In 2014, she achieved a lifelong dream by winning the Surf 'n' Sea Pipeline Women's Pro in Hawaii. Her unwavering determination and incredible achievements have made her a role model for aspiring surfers and anyone facing adversity.

TWO

In addition to her success in the surfing world, Bethany has used her platform to advocate for numerous causes, including environmental conservation, clean water initiatives, and helping people with disabilities access adaptive sports. Through her work, she has impacted countless lives and inspired others to recalibrate their perspectives and embrace their challenges as opportunities for growth.

Bethany Hamilton's story is a testament to the power of recalibration, resilience, and the human spirit. Despite losing her arm to a shark attack at the age of 13, she has achieved incredible success in the world of professional surfing and has used her experience to inspire millions of people around the globe. Her journey serves as a reminder that when we face adversity, we can choose to recalibrate our perspectives and use our challenges to our advantage, turning our struggles into the fuel that drives us towards greatness.

Bethany's journey did not stop with her achievements in the world of surfing. As she transitioned into new phases of life, she continued to inspire and motivate others. She married her husband, Adam Dirks, in 2013, and together they have welcomed two beautiful children into the world. This new chapter in her life has further demonstrated her ability to adapt and overcome challenges, as she balances motherhood and her continued work as an advocate and role model.

In 2018, Bethany released a documentary titled "Unstoppable," which chronicled her life's journey from the shark attack to her incredible accomplishments in surfing and beyond. The documentary provided an intimate look into her life, showcasing her strength, determination, and unbreakable spirit.

As a motivational speaker, Bethany continues to travel the world, sharing her story and empowering others to embrace their own challenges and persevere in the face of adversity. Through her message, she encourages her audiences to recalibrate their own perspectives, to see their challenges not as insurmountable obstacles but as opportunities for growth and self-discovery.

Bethany's impact extends far beyond the world of surfing. Her story has inspired countless people facing adversity in various forms, from physical disabilities to emotional struggles. She has demonstrated that, with faith, determination, and a willingness to recalibrate one's perspective, it is possible to overcome even the most daunting challenges and achieve greatness.

In conclusion, the story of Bethany Hamilton is an inspiring example of the power of recalibration, resilience, and the human spirit. Despite losing her arm in a shark attack at a young age, she has been able to transform her adversity into a powerful platform to inspire and uplift others. Her life serves as a reminder that when we face challenges, we can choose to recalibrate our perspectives and use them to our advantage, turning our struggles into the fuel that drives us toward greatness.

THREE
SCALING NEW HEIGHTS - THE REMARKABLE STORY OF ERIK WEIHENMAYER

Erik Weihenmayer, born on September 23, 1968, in Princeton, New Jersey, is a world-class adventurer, athlete, and motivational speaker. Despite losing his vision at the age of 13 due to a degenerative eye condition called retinoschisis, Erik refused to let this setback define his life. Instead, he recalibrated his approach and used adversity to his advantage, becoming the first blind person to summit Mount Everest and complete the Seven Summits.

From a young age, Erik faced the harsh reality of his deteriorating vision. His world gradually turned dark, forcing him to navigate the challenges of growing up without sight. However, Erik was determined to push beyond his limitations and embrace the world of adventure that awaited him. With the support of his family, Erik enrolled in a school for the blind, where he learned critical skills such as Braille and mobility with a white cane.

During his teenage years, Erik discovered a passion for rock climbing. With the guidance of his coach and mentor, he developed techniques to scale climbing walls and mountains despite his blindness. Erik learned to rely on tactile cues, such as feeling the rock's contours with his hands, and auditory cues, such as listening to his climbing partners' verbal guidance, to navigate the vertical terrain.

As Erik honed his climbing skills, he realized that his blindness could be an asset rather than a hindrance. His heightened senses of touch and hearing allowed him to perceive the rock formations differently from sighted climbers, providing him with a unique perspective on the challenges he faced. Inspired by this newfound strength, Erik set his sights on Mount Everest, the tallest mountain in the world.

In 2001, after years of intense training and preparation, Erik embarked on his historic Everest expedition. Accompanied by a team of experienced climbers, Erik used his remarkable ability to adapt to the unpredictable mountain environment. He faced numerous dangers, including treacherous icefalls, thin air, and exhaustion. Yet, with each challenge, Erik recalibrated his approach, learning from his mistakes and pushing onward.

On May 25, 2001, Erik's perseverance paid off as he stood on the summit of Mount Everest, proving that even the most insurmountable obstacles could be conquered. His achievement garnered worldwide attention and inspired countless individuals facing their own adversities.

Erik's journey didn't end with Everest. He went on to complete the Seven Summits, the highest peak on each continent, and founded No Barriers, a nonprofit organization that empowers people with disabilities to break through their perceived limitations and achieve greatness.

After conquering the Seven Summits, Erik continued to push the boundaries of what was thought possible for a blind person. He took on a new challenge: kayaking. Despite the risks involved, especially for someone without sight, Erik embraced this new adventure with the same determination and spirit he had shown throughout his life.

In 2014, Erik embarked on an extraordinary mission to kayak the entire 277 miles of the Colorado River through the Grand Canyon. To prepare for this daunting task, he trained extensively, learning to rely on auditory cues to navigate the treacherous rapids. Erik's kayaking guide would call out instructions, allowing him to react quickly and avoid potential dangers. This new way of experiencing the river provided Erik with a fresh perspective on the power of resilience and recalibration.

The journey through the Grand Canyon was anything but easy. The river's powerful currents, hidden rocks, and unpredictable rapids challenged Erik and his team at every turn. However, despite the ever-present dangers and the intense physical demands of the journey, Erik persevered, displaying the same indomitable spirit that had carried him to the summit of Everest.

On September 28, 2014, after 21 days of intense kayaking, Erik successfully completed his journey through the Grand Canyon. His accomplishment once again demonstrated the power of recalibration and the limitless potential of the human spirit. Erik's story inspired countless people to face their own adversities with courage, determination, and resilience.

Today, Erik Weihenmayer continues to break barriers and redefine what is possible for people with disabilities. He travels the world as a motivational speaker, sharing his story and empowering others to overcome their own obstacles. Through his work with No Barriers, Erik has transformed the lives of thousands of individuals, helping them to discover their potential and embrace the power of recalibration.

Erik Weihenmayer's remarkable journey is a testament to the human spirit's resilience and the transformative power of recalibration. His story teaches us that we can overcome even the most significant challenges if we are willing to adapt, learn, and persevere. By refusing to let adversity hold him back, Erik has become a beacon of hope and inspiration for countless people across the globe, proving that the only true barriers are those we place on ourselves.

FOUR
FROM CIVIL RIGHTS ACTIVIST TO CONGRESSWOMAN: THE INSPIRING JOURNEY OF BARBARA LEE

Reading about Barbara Lee's life and accomplishments has left me feeling incredibly inspired and motivated. As someone who has also faced obstacles in pursuing my passions and goals, I can relate to the challenges that she has had to overcome as a Black woman in politics.

Barbara Lee is a Democratic politician who has been a fierce advocate for civil rights, social justice, and progressive causes throughout her career. Born in El Paso, Texas in 1946, Lee grew up in a military family and spent much of her childhood traveling the world. Her exposure to different cultures and experiences would shape her perspective and inform her activism in later life.

Lee attended college at Mills College in Oakland, California, where she became involved in the civil rights movement and anti-war protests. Her activism continued after college, as she began working as a community organizer and advocate for marginalized communities. She fought for racial justice, women's rights, and economic equality, working for various nonprofit organizations and serving as a staff member for Congressman Ron Dellums, who represented Oakland and surrounding areas.

In 1998, Lee made history by becoming the first Black woman elected to Congress from Northern California. During her tenure in Congress, Lee has been a vocal and passionate advocate for a range of progressive causes. She has fought for equal rights for women and LGBTQ+ people, championed efforts to combat poverty and homelessness, and worked to end the war on drugs and reform the criminal justice system.

Perhaps Lee's most notable achievement was her vote against the Authorization for Use of Military Force Against Terrorists, which was passed by Congress in the aftermath of the September 11th attacks. Lee was the only member of Congress to vote against the measure, which authorized the use of military force in Afghanistan and has been used as the legal basis for U.S. military interventions around the world. Lee's vote was a courageous stand against war and militarism, and has cemented her legacy as a fearless and principled leader.

Throughout her career, Lee has been recognized for her work and leadership. She has received numerous awards and

FOUR

honors, including the NAACP's Rosa Parks Award and the National Organization for Women's Woman of Courage Award. In 2020, she was appointed as a co-chair of the Biden-Harris transition team, reflecting her status as a respected and influential voice within the Democratic Party.

Barbara Lee's journey to Congress is a testament to the power of activism, determination, and leadership. Her commitment to social justice and progressive causes has inspired countless others to join the fight for a better world. Her legacy serves as a reminder that change is possible, even in the face of seemingly insurmountable challenges.

In addition to her work in Congress, Lee has also been a strong advocate for international peace and cooperation. She has traveled extensively around the world, meeting with leaders and activists in various countries and working to promote peace and human rights. She has served as a member of the United States delegation to the United Nations and has worked on issues such as global health, women's rights, and international development.

Throughout her career, Lee has remained committed to her values and principles, even in the face of criticism and opposition. She has been a vocal critic of the Trump administration's policies, including its efforts to dismantle the Affordable Care Act and its treatment of immigrants and refugees. She has also been a strong supporter of the Black Lives Matter movement and has worked to address issues of police brutality and systemic racism.

As she continues to serve in Congress, Lee remains committed to advancing progressive policies and fighting for the marginalized and vulnerable. Her story is a reminder of the power of leadership and activism in bringing about positive change in the world. Her legacy will inspire generations to come to continue the fight for justice, equality, and human rights.

Lee's influence has also extended beyond her district and party. She has worked to build bridges and collaborate with colleagues across the aisle to find common ground and advance important issues. She has been recognized for her bipartisanship and ability to work with colleagues on both sides of the aisle, particularly on issues related to poverty and hunger.

In addition to her work in Congress, Lee has also been involved in various philanthropic and charitable organizations. She has served on the boards of several nonprofits, including the Congressional Hunger Center and the California Black Women's Health Project, and has worked to promote access to education and healthcare for underserved communities.

Lee's journey to Congress has been one marked by courage, dedication, and a fierce commitment to justice and equality. She has been a trailblazer and an inspiration to many, particularly to young women and people of color. Her legacy will continue to shape the future of politics and activism for generations to come.

Barbara Lee's story serves as a powerful reminder of the importance of representation in politics. As a Black woman in a historically male-dominated field, Lee has fought for greater diversity and inclusion in Congress and the political sphere more broadly. She has been a vocal advocate for increasing the number of women and people of color in elected office, and has worked to promote policies that benefit marginalized and vulnerable communities.

Her leadership and advocacy have earned her the respect and admiration of colleagues and constituents alike. She has been recognized as one of the most effective and influential members of Congress, and her legacy continues to inspire and motivate activists and leaders around the world.

As she continues to serve in Congress, Lee remains committed to fighting for a more just and equitable society. She has called for bold action to address issues such as climate change, economic inequality, and racial justice, and has worked to build coalitions and partnerships to advance these important causes.

Barbara Lee's journey is a testament to the power of leadership, activism, and advocacy. Her story serves as an inspiration to all those who aspire to make a difference in the world, and a reminder that even the most daunting challenges can be overcome with courage, determination, and a steadfast commitment to justice and equality.

FIVE
SCALING THE HEIGHTS - THE STORY OF ARUNIMA SINHA

Arunima Sinha was born on July 20, 1988, in the Ambedkar Nagar District of Uttar Pradesh, India. Life took an unexpected turn when she was just 23 years old. Arunima, a former national-level volleyball player, lost her leg in a tragic accident. However, her story is one of incredible recalibration, resilience, and triumph over adversity, as she went on to become the first female amputee to climb Mount Everest.

On April 11, 2011, Arunima was traveling by train from Lucknow to Delhi when a group of thieves attempted to rob her. During the struggle, she was pushed from the moving train and fell onto the tracks. Her left leg was severely injured and had to be amputated below the knee. The accident was a turning point in her life, but Arunima refused to let it define her.

Following the incident, Arunima recalibrated her goals and decided to take up mountaineering. She knew the challenges she faced would be immense, but her determination to turn her adversity into an opportunity for growth propelled her forward. She trained at the Nehru Institute of Mountaineering in Uttarkashi under the guidance of Bachendri Pal, the first Indian woman to climb Mount Everest.

Arunima faced countless hurdles, from physical limitations to financial constraints, but she remained steadfast in her pursuit of her dream. In May 2013, just two years after losing her leg, Arunima achieved the seemingly impossible: she scaled Mount Everest, becoming the first female amputee to do so.

Her extraordinary feat was widely celebrated and brought attention to the immense potential of people with disabilities. Arunima continued to recalibrate her goals, setting her sights on scaling the highest peaks on each continent. She went on to conquer several more mountains, including Kilimanjaro in Africa, Elbrus in Europe, Kosciuszko in Australia, and Aconcagua in South America.

Arunima's journey is a shining example of the transformative power of recalibration. By reassessing her goals and the path to achieving them, she was able to rise above her challenges and become a symbol of hope, strength, and perseverance. Her story teaches us that no matter what circumstances we find ourselves in, we have the power to change our trajectory and achieve greatness.

SIX
RISING FROM THE ASHES - THE RESILIENT JOURNEY OF TURIA PITT

Turia Pitt, born on July 24, 1987, in Ulladulla, Australia, is a motivational speaker, author, and athlete. A survivor of a near-fatal accident, Turia's story of recalibration and resilience in the face of adversity has inspired countless individuals around the world.

In 2011, Turia's life changed forever when she was caught in a bushfire during an ultramarathon race in Western Australia's Kimberley region. The fire engulfed her, leaving her with severe burns to 65% of her body. Turia was airlifted to a hospital, where she was placed in a medically induced coma for a month.

Turia's prognosis was grim. She had to undergo over 200 surgeries, including amputations of several fingers and a thumb, and countless hours of grueling physical therapy. The once fiercely independent young woman now depended on others for her most basic needs. Despite the overwhelming physical and emotional challenges, Turia was determined to regain her strength and independence.

During her recovery, Turia displayed an unyielding spirit of recalibration. She embraced her new reality and refused to let the accident define her. Turia set a series of ambitious goals for herself, including completing an Ironman triathlon and raising funds for the non-profit organization, Interplast, which provides reconstructive surgery for people in developing countries.

Turia's path to achieving these goals was anything but smooth. Her physical therapy sessions were often excruciating, and she faced numerous setbacks in her recovery. Nevertheless, Turia's determination to rebuild her life never wavered.

In 2016, just five years after her accident, Turia achieved her goal of completing an Ironman triathlon in Port Macquarie, Australia. She swam 2.4 miles, biked 112 miles, and ran 26.2 miles, a remarkable feat for anyone, let alone someone who had endured the challenges Turia faced. Her accomplishment garnered international attention and demonstrated the power of recalibration and resilience in overcoming adversity.

Turia has also made significant strides in her philanthropic work. She has raised over a million dollars for Interplast, helping to fund life-changing surgeries for those in need. She has become an influential motivational speaker, sharing her story with audiences worldwide and encouraging others to embrace the power of recalibration in their own lives.

Furthermore, Turia has written several books detailing her journey, including "Everything to Live For" and "Unmasked." In these books, Turia shares the raw, honest account of her struggles and triumphs, providing readers with a unique perspective on resilience and the human spirit's capacity to overcome obstacles. Her refusal to let her circumstances dictate her future serves as an inspiration to others facing their own challenges.

By sharing her story and her commitment to helping others, Turia has demonstrated that, with determination, courage, and the willingness to adapt, we can rise above even the most significant obstacles and achieve greatness.

SEVEN
OVERCOMING FAILURE - THE JOURNEY OF FRIDA KAHLO TO ARTISTIC GREATNESS

Frida Kahlo is one of the most celebrated and iconic artists of the 20th century, known for her bold and vivid self-portraits and her groundbreaking exploration of identity, gender, and Mexican culture. However, her journey to artistic greatness was marked by numerous challenges and obstacles, which she overcame through resilience, creativity, and a steadfast commitment to her vision.

Kahlo was born in Mexico City in 1907, the daughter of a German father and a Mexican mother. She grew up in a politically and culturally tumultuous time, and her childhood was marked by illness and physical disabilities, including polio and a severe bus accident at the age of 18 that left her with lifelong chronic pain and disabilities.

Despite her physical challenges, Kahlo showed an early talent for art and began painting seriously after the accident. She drew on her own experiences and emotions to create deeply personal and expressive works, often featuring vivid self-portraits and depictions of Mexican culture and folklore.

Kahlo faced numerous obstacles in her artistic career, including discrimination and sexism in the male-dominated art world. However, she remained determined to share her vision and her voice with the world, and eventually gained recognition and acclaim for her work.

Kahlo's journey was also marked by personal challenges and setbacks, including a tumultuous marriage to fellow artist Diego Rivera, who was unfaithful and emotionally abusive. Despite the challenges of her personal life, Kahlo continued to create art that spoke to her experiences and her struggles, and her work has become an inspiration to generations of artists and activists around the world.

As she continued to explore her art and her identity, Kahlo became a powerful voice for women, minorities, and marginalized communities. She used her platform to advocate for social justice and equality, and her work continues to inspire and empower people around the world to this day.

Kahlo's journey to recalibration was one of resilience, creativity, and a steadfast commitment to her vision and her values. Despite the challenges and obstacles she faced, she remained true to herself and her art, creating works that spoke to the deepest parts of the human experience. Her legacy serves as an inspiration to all those who aspire to greatness, and a reminder that even in the face of adversity, creativity and self-expression can be a powerful tool for change and transformation.

Kahlo's influence on the art world and beyond continues to be felt to this day. Her work has been exhibited in museums and galleries around the world, and has been the subject of numerous books, films, and documentaries. Her unique style and perspective have inspired generations of artists, particularly women and people of color, to explore their own experiences and identities through art.

In addition to her artistic legacy, Kahlo's life and work have become a symbol of resilience, strength, and empowerment. Her willingness to share her own struggles and challenges through her art has inspired countless individuals to confront their own difficulties and to find their own voices and identities.

Kahlo's journey is a powerful example of the importance of recalibration and self-expression in overcoming adversity. Her story serves as an inspiration to all those who face challenges and obstacles in life, and a reminder that through creativity, resilience, and determination, even the most daunting challenges can be overcome.

EIGHT
DEFYING GRAVITY - THE COURAGEOUS STORY OF JESSICA COX

Jessica Cox, born on February 2, 1983, in Tucson, Arizona, is an extraordinary individual who has faced and overcome significant challenges in her life. Born without arms due to a rare birth defect called amelia, Jessica has embraced her uniqueness and defied all expectations by becoming the first armless pilot, a motivational speaker, and an advocate for people with disabilities.

From an early age, Jessica faced numerous obstacles. Growing up without arms meant she had to learn to perform daily tasks using her feet. Her parents, determined to provide her with a sense of normalcy, refused to treat her differently from her siblings. Jessica learned to eat, write, and even play the piano using her feet. Despite the challenges she faced, she was determined not to let her disability define her or limit her potential.

Jessica's interest in aviation began when she was a child, inspired by her father's love for flying. However, her dream of becoming a pilot seemed unattainable due to her disability. After years of convincing herself that flying was not in her future, she encountered a life-changing opportunity: meeting a pilot with a disability who encouraged her to pursue her dream.

Determined to defy gravity, Jessica embarked on a journey to learn how to fly. Using a specially modified aircraft called the Ercoupe, which did not require the use of hands to operate, she began her flight training. Jessica faced numerous challenges, from adapting to the unique controls to mastering the complex maneuvers required to pilot an aircraft. She learned to recalibrate her approach to flying, using her feet and legs to perform the tasks most pilots do with their hands.

In 2008, after three years of hard work and determination, Jessica made history by becoming the first armless person to earn a pilot's license. Her achievement garnered international attention and served as a powerful testament to the power of recalibration and the resilience of the human spirit.

Jessica's accomplishments did not stop there. She became a certified scuba diver, a black belt in Taekwondo, and an advocate for people with disabilities. As a motivational speaker, she shares her story with audiences worldwide, inspiring them to embrace their unique abilities and overcome their personal obstacles.

In 2009, Jessica's story caught the attention of filmmaker Nick Spark, who decided to create a documentary about her life, called "Right Footed." The documentary showcased Jessica's journey from a child struggling with her disability to an accomplished pilot and motivational speaker. It also highlighted her work as a mentor and advocate for people with disabilities, particularly children, inspiring them to pursue their dreams and overcome adversity.

Jessica's impact extends beyond her achievements as a pilot and her work as a motivational speaker. She has also used her influence to raise awareness about the challenges faced by people with disabilities worldwide. In 2013, she was appointed as a Goodwill Ambassador for Humanity & Inclusion (formerly Handicap International), a non-profit organization dedicated to supporting people with disabilities in developing countries. In this role, she has traveled to countries such as Ethiopia and the Philippines to promote disability rights, inclusion, and empowerment.

One of Jessica's most significant accomplishments has been the establishment of the Jessica Cox Motivation and Training Center in the Philippines. The center, which she co-founded with her husband, Patrick Chamberlain, aims to empower individuals with disabilities and provide them with the necessary resources and support to excel in various aspects of life, including education, employment, and sports.

Jessica's tireless advocacy for disability rights has not gone unnoticed. In 2015, she received the Inspiration Award at the first-ever Filipino-American History Month Celebration at the White House. The accolade recognized her exceptional achievements and her dedication to making a positive impact on the lives of people with disabilities.

Jessica Cox's extraordinary story continues to inspire countless individuals worldwide, demonstrating the transformative power of recalibration and resilience in the face of adversity. Her determination to overcome her disability and embrace her unique abilities has not only allowed her to achieve greatness but also to become a symbol of hope for those facing their own challenges. Through her advocacy work, mentorship, and motivational speaking, Jessica has shown that with the right mindset and support, anyone can defy the odds and achieve their dreams.

NINE
AN UNBREAKABLE WILL - THE REMARKABLE STORY OF DR. SAKENA YACOOBI

Dr. Sakena Yacoobi, born in 1948 in Herat, Afghanistan, is an extraordinary woman who has devoted her life to empowering women and children through education. Despite facing immense personal challenges and living through the turbulence of war and the oppressive Taliban regime, she has successfully established schools, training centers, and clinics in Afghanistan, transforming the lives of countless individuals.

Sakena's passion for education was evident from a young age. Growing up in a middle-class family in Afghanistan, she was fortunate to receive an education, a privilege often denied to many girls. After completing her bachelor's degree in Kabul, she moved to the United States for further studies, eventually earning a Master's degree in Public Health from Loma Linda University.

In 1992, Sakena founded the Afghan Institute of Learning (AIL), an organization dedicated to providing education and healthcare to Afghan women and children. The timing could not have been more challenging; Afghanistan was in the midst of a brutal civil war, and the situation worsened with the rise of the Taliban regime in 1996.

Under the Taliban, women and girls were systematically denied access to education, healthcare, and employment. Sakena's work suddenly became illegal and life-threatening. However, she was determined to continue her mission to empower women and children. It was at this moment that she embraced the idea of recalibration, using the adversity she faced to her advantage.

Sakena began secretly establishing underground schools for girls, disguised as sewing classes or other acceptable activities. She trained female teachers to provide education in the privacy of their homes, often at great personal risk. In a society where women were beaten or even killed for seeking knowledge, Sakena's determination and courage were truly remarkable.

As the Taliban's control weakened, Sakena expanded AIL's efforts, establishing schools, training centers, and clinics in Afghanistan. AIL's programs focus on education, healthcare, leadership development, and human rights, with the goal of empowering women and children to become agents of change in their communities. Over the years, AIL has provided education and services to millions of Afghans, transforming lives and giving hope to those who had been denied access to basic human rights.

Sakena's work has not gone unnoticed. She has received numerous international awards and accolades for her tireless efforts, including the Opus Prize, the WISE Prize for Education, and the Sunhak Peace Prize. In 2015, she was nominated for the Nobel Peace Prize, a testament to the profound impact she has made on the lives of countless Afghans.

In addition to her work with the Afghan Institute of Learning, Dr. Sakena Yacoobi has actively collaborated with international organizations to raise awareness about the importance of education and women's rights in Afghanistan. She has spoken at numerous conferences, including the United Nations, the Clinton Global Initiative, and the World Economic Forum, sharing her experiences and the challenges she faced in her quest to empower women and children through education.

Sakena's impact on the lives of Afghan women and children is immeasurable. Her schools and training centers have equipped thousands of individuals with the skills, knowledge, and confidence to pursue better lives for themselves and their families. Many of her students have become teachers, health workers, and entrepreneurs, contributing to the development of their communities and the rebuilding of their country.

One of the key components of Sakena's educational approach is the emphasis on critical thinking, problem-solving, and leadership development. She believes that true empowerment comes from the ability to question and challenge the status quo, and to take charge of one's own destiny. By fostering these skills in her students, she has helped to create a new generation of change-makers in Afghanistan, who are better equipped to face the challenges that lie ahead.

Sakena's work has also inspired others to take up the cause of education and women's rights in Afghanistan and beyond. Her success has shown that change is possible, even in the most difficult and oppressive circumstances, and that the power of education can transform lives and communities.

As Afghanistan faces a new set of challenges in the wake of the recent political upheaval, Sakena's legacy of courage, determination, and resilience serves as a beacon of hope for those who continue to fight for the rights of women and children. Despite the uncertainty and adversity that lie ahead, her life's work stands as a testament to the transformative power of education and the indomitable human spirit.

Dr. Sakena Yacoobi's remarkable story is a shining example of how one person's determination to recalibrate their approach in the face of adversity can have a profound and lasting impact on countless lives. Her unwavering commitment to the cause of education and women's empowerment in Afghanistan serves as an inspiration to all who strive to make a positive difference in the world, reminding us that even in the darkest times, hope and resilience can prevail.

TEN
RISING FROM THE SHADOWS - THE MAGICAL JOURNEY OF J.K. ROWLING

Joanne Rowling, better known as J.K. Rowling, was born on July 31, 1965, in Yate, England. Her journey to becoming one of the most successful and influential authors in history was riddled with adversity, but through resilience, recalibration, and determination, she transformed her life and inspired millions.

Rowling's love for storytelling began at a young age, and she started writing her first stories when she was just six years old. However, her journey to becoming a published author was far from smooth. After graduating from the University of Exeter, Rowling found herself in a series of unfulfilling jobs, while still nurturing her passion for writing.

Her idea for the Harry Potter series came to her during a train journey from Manchester to London in 1990. Over the next several years, she meticulously outlined the entire series and began writing the first book, "Harry Potter and the Philosopher's Stone." During this time, Rowling's life took a series of challenging turns. She moved to Portugal, where she got married and had a daughter. However, her marriage soon ended in divorce, and she returned to the United Kingdom as a single mother, struggling to make ends meet.

Rowling continued to work on her manuscript while navigating life as a single parent and living on state benefits. She faced numerous rejections from publishers, but she didn't allow these setbacks to deter her. Instead, she recalibrated her approach and continued to pursue her dream of becoming a published author.

In 1997, Rowling's persistence finally paid off when her manuscript was accepted by Bloomsbury Publishing. "Harry Potter and the Philosopher's Stone" was published later that year, marking the beginning of a global phenomenon that would change her life and the lives of millions of readers.

The Harry Potter series went on to become one of the most successful book franchises in history, selling over 500 million copies worldwide and translated into more than 80 languages. The books were also adapted into a highly successful film series, further solidifying Rowling's status as a cultural icon.

Throughout her journey, J.K. Rowling exemplified the power of recalibration and resilience. Her story demonstrates that, in the face of adversity, one can choose to adapt and persevere, ultimately achieving great success. Rowling's unwavering determination and belief in her abilities allowed her to overcome the many obstacles that stood in her way.

TEN

Rowling's success also enabled her to become a philanthropist and advocate for numerous causes. She founded the Volant Charitable Trust, which supports organizations that address social deprivation, as well as the international children's charity, Lumos, which works to end the institutionalization of children worldwide. Her advocacy and charitable work further illustrate her dedication to using her success to make a positive impact on the world.

J.K. Rowling's journey serves as a powerful reminder of the power of recalibration and resilience in the face of adversity. Her story demonstrates that even the most seemingly insurmountable challenges can be overcome with determination, courage, and an unwavering belief in one's ability to create change.

In a world where many people face adversity and struggle, J.K. Rowling's story offers hope and inspiration. By sharing her journey, she encourages others to recalibrate their own perspectives, to view their challenges not as insurmountable obstacles but as opportunities for growth and self-discovery.

As we face our own challenges, let us remember the incredible story of J.K. Rowling and the power of recalibration. Let us recognize that we, too, can transform our lives by choosing to view our struggles as opportunities for growth and by embracing the resilience that lies within each of us. Through our own determination and perseverance, we can carry on the legacy of J.K. Rowling, using adversity to our advantage and achieving greatness in the face of seemingly insurmountable odds.

Rowling's journey is a shining example of the transformative power of recalibration. By reassessing her goals and the path to achieving them, she was able to rise above her challenges and become a symbol of hope, strength, and perseverance. Her story teaches us that no matter what circumstances we find ourselves in, we have the power to change our trajectory and achieve greatness.

By sharing her story, she has inspired countless individuals to face their own challenges head-on, using adversity to their advantage and creating lives filled with purpose and success.

ELEVEN
TURNING THE TIDE - THE INSPIRING STORY OF JOÃO CARLOS MARTINS

João Carlos Martins is a name that is not well-known outside the world of classical music. Yet, his story is one of unparalleled resilience and determination in the face of adversity. A Brazilian pianist and conductor, Martins has turned the tide on his misfortunes and recalibrated his life to achieve greatness.

Born in 1940, Martins began playing the piano at the age of eight. By the time he was 18, he had already gained international recognition as a piano prodigy. With a blossoming career ahead of him, he was quickly becoming one of the leading pianists of his generation. However, fate had other plans.

In 1965, a soccer accident left Martins with a severe injury to his right arm. His doctors warned him that he might never regain full use of his arm again, which could mean the end of his career as a pianist. But Martins was not one to give up easily. He recalibrated his approach to playing, focusing on developing his left-hand technique, and resumed performing concerts.

Unfortunately, this was not the last of the obstacles Martins would face. In 1972, a neurological condition began to affect his hand control, forcing him to retire from piano performance. Once again, Martins recalibrated his life, this time by turning to conducting. He studied under some of the most renowned conductors and became a successful conductor himself, leading orchestras around the world.

However, in 1995, Martins faced yet another setback when he was mugged and beaten, resulting in further damage to his hands and his ability to conduct. The following year, a brain tumor and subsequent surgery caused even more complications. It seemed that fate was determined to keep Martins from his passion for music.

But Martins refused to give in. He persevered through multiple surgeries and extensive physical therapy, recalibrating his approach to music once more. In 2003, he founded the Bachiana Filarmônica, a Brazilian orchestra composed of young musicians from underprivileged backgrounds. Martins used his talent and experience to help these young musicians develop their skills and find success in the world of classical music.

In 2019, at the age of 79, Martins received a pair of bionic gloves designed by an industrial designer, which enabled him to play the piano again. The gloves provided the necessary support to his fingers, allowing him to regain some control over his hand movements. With this newfound ability, Martins returned to the piano, performing once more for audiences around the world.

In recent years, João Carlos Martins has become a symbol of resilience and hope, inspiring countless people through his unwavering dedication to his art. His story has also been the subject of a biographical film, "João, O Maestro," which premiered in 2017, bringing his incredible journey to the big screen and introducing his story to a wider audience.

As Martins' story gained prominence, his impact extended far beyond the realm of classical music. He began to use his influence to advocate for accessibility and opportunities for people with disabilities, pushing for the creation of new technologies and resources to help them overcome their challenges. His own experiences with bionic gloves have shown the potential of innovative solutions to change lives, and Martins has made it his mission to help others benefit from similar advancements.

In addition to his work with the Bachiana Filarmônica, Martins has also been involved in various charitable initiatives and educational programs. He has established music schools in underprivileged communities across Brazil, providing children with access to quality music education and fostering a new generation of talented musicians. Through these efforts, Martins has not only changed the lives of countless young musicians but also enriched the cultural landscape of his country.

For João Carlos Martins, the numerous setbacks and obstacles he has faced in his life have only served to strengthen his resolve and fuel his passion for music. He has continuously adapted and recalibrated his approach to overcome adversity, proving that no challenge is insurmountable with determination and the willingness to adapt. His story serves as a powerful reminder that even in the face of seemingly insurmountable challenges, it is possible to persevere, reinvent ourselves, and ultimately triumph.

Today, Martins continues to conduct, perform, and inspire. His story of resilience and adaptation in the face of adversity serves as a powerful example for people around the world, demonstrating that it is not our circumstances that define us but our ability to adapt and overcome. As João Carlos Martins' life and career continue to evolve, his indomitable spirit and unwavering commitment to his art stand as a testament to the power of recalibration and the enduring strength of the human spirit.

TWELVE
RISING ABOVE - THE STORY OF STEPHEN HAWKING

Stephen Hawking was born on January 8, 1942, in Oxford, England. Despite being diagnosed with amyotrophic lateral sclerosis (ALS) at the age of 21, a progressive neurodegenerative disease that left him almost entirely paralyzed, his story is one of incredible recalibration, resilience, and triumph over adversity. Hawking went on to become one of the most renowned theoretical physicists and cosmologists in history.

Hawking's journey began when he was a student at the University of Cambridge, working towards his Ph.D. in cosmology. It was during this time that he was diagnosed with ALS, a disease that would gradually rob him of his ability to move, speak, and even breathe. The doctors gave him a life expectancy of just two years. Despite the devastating prognosis, Hawking refused to let his diagnosis define him or his future.

Faced with this unimaginable challenge, Hawking recalibrated his approach to life and his work. He chose to focus on the things he could still do, rather than dwelling on his limitations. He continued his studies, determined to make groundbreaking contributions to the field of theoretical physics.

His perseverance paid off. Hawking's work on black holes, specifically his discovery of Hawking radiation, revolutionized our understanding of the universe. He went on to become a professor at Cambridge, where he held the prestigious Lucasian Chair of Mathematics, a position once held by Sir Isaac Newton.

In addition to his groundbreaking scientific work, Hawking became an advocate for people with disabilities. He used his platform to raise awareness and funds for research into neurodegenerative diseases, like ALS, and to challenge misconceptions about the capabilities of those living with disabilities.

Hawking's ability to recalibrate his perspective and adapt to his circumstances proved to be the key to his success. He continued to work, write, and communicate, despite his physical limitations, through the use of a computer-based communication system that allowed him to speak using a speech synthesizer.

Stephen Hawking's accomplishments did not stop there. He went on to become a prolific author, penning numerous books, including the bestselling "A Brief History of Time." He also appeared on various television programs and documentaries, further cementing his status as a cultural icon and an inspiration to millions.

Throughout his life, Hawking continued to recalibrate his approach to communication and advocacy, using his own experiences as a catalyst for change. He traveled the world, giving speeches and lectures that inspired millions and shed light on the challenges faced by people with disabilities. He also worked tirelessly to raise funds and awareness for organizations such as the Motor Neurone Disease Association and the Stephen Hawking Foundation.

His story demonstrates that even the most seemingly insurmountable challenges can be overcome with determination, courage, and an unwavering belief in one's ability to create change.

THIRTEEN
FROM TRAGEDY TO TRIUMPH - THE STORY OF MALALA YOUSAFZAI

Malala Yousafzai was born on July 12, 1997, in Mingora, Swat District, Pakistan. She grew up in a region where education for girls was often restricted by conservative cultural norms and the oppressive rule of the Taliban. Despite the significant challenges she faced, Malala's story is one of extraordinary recalibration, resilience, and triumph over adversity, as she dedicated her life to advocating for the right to education for girls around the world.

Malala's journey began with the support and encouragement of her father, Ziauddin Yousafzai, an educator and advocate for girls' education. He instilled in her the importance of learning and the power of knowledge, sparking her passion for education and her commitment to fighting for the rights of girls everywhere.

As the Taliban's control over the Swat Valley tightened, they began closing schools and banning girls from attending. Malala, just a young girl at the time, refused to be silenced by their oppressive rule. She began writing an anonymous blog for the BBC, documenting her experiences under the Taliban's rule and her determination to continue her education despite the risks.

Malala's courage and dedication soon caught the attention of the international community, making her a target for the Taliban. On October 9, 2012, when she was only 15 years old, Malala was shot by a Taliban gunman while on her way home from school. The attack left her in critical condition, but her indomitable spirit would not be broken.

Following the attack, Malala was flown to Birmingham, UK, for specialized medical treatment. She spent months in the hospital, undergoing multiple surgeries and extensive rehabilitation. During this time, Malala used her experience to recalibrate her perspective and strengthen her resolve to fight for the right to education for girls around the world.

As Malala recovered, her story became a symbol of hope and resilience for millions of people worldwide. Her determination to turn tragedy into an opportunity for growth and advocacy inspired countless individuals to join her in the fight for girls' education.

Upon her recovery, Malala and her family relocated to the UK, where she continued her education and advocacy work. In 2013, she co-authored the memoir "I Am Malala:

THIRTEEN

The Girl Who Stood Up for Education and Was Shot by the Taliban," which became an international bestseller and further amplified her message.

Malala's unwavering commitment to her cause soon garnered recognition on the global stage. In 2014, at the age of 17, she became the youngest-ever recipient of the Nobel Peace Prize, in recognition of her efforts to promote education and women's rights.

With her newfound platform, Malala continued to recalibrate her approach to advocacy, expanding her focus to include the broader issues of girls' education, gender equality, and human rights. In 2015, she established the Malala Fund, a nonprofit organization dedicated to breaking down the barriers that prevent girls from accessing quality education.

By sharing her story, she has inspired countless individuals to face their own challenges head-on, using adversity to their advantage and creating lives filled with purpose and success. As we face our own struggles, let us remember the power of recalibration and the inspiring story of Malala Yousafzai, using her example as a beacon of hope and motivation in our journey towards greatness.

FOURTEEN
THE UNBREAKABLE SPIRIT - THE STORY OF NELSON MANDELA

Nelson Mandela was born on July 18, 1918, in the village of Qunu, South Africa. He grew up in a time of racial segregation and oppression, where the white minority ruled over the black majority through a system of strict laws and regulations known as apartheid. Despite the immense challenges he faced, Mandela's story would become one of remarkable recalibration, resilience, and triumph over adversity, as he dedicated his life to the pursuit of freedom and equality for all South Africans.

Mandela's journey began when he moved to Johannesburg to study law and later joined the African National Congress (ANC), a political organization dedicated to fighting for the rights of black South Africans. As the apartheid regime's oppressive policies continued to escalate, Mandela and the

ANC resorted to more radical means of resistance, including acts of sabotage against the government.

In 1962, Mandela was arrested and charged with conspiracy to overthrow the state, a crime punishable by death. However, during his trial, Mandela used the courtroom as a platform to speak out against the injustices of apartheid, garnering international attention and support. He was ultimately sentenced to life imprisonment and spent the next 27 years behind bars, mostly in the notorious Robben Island prison.

Despite the harsh conditions of his imprisonment, Mandela remained steadfast in his commitment to ending apartheid and achieving a just and equal society. He used his time in prison to recalibrate his perspective, focusing on the long-term goals of freedom and democracy for South Africa, even when the odds seemed insurmountable.

Mandela's unwavering dedication to his cause soon made him a symbol of hope and resilience for millions of South Africans and people around the world. His ability to recalibrate his life in the face of adversity and remain steadfast in his pursuit of justice inspired countless individuals to join the fight against apartheid.

Throughout his time in prison, Mandela continued to engage in negotiations with the South African government, seeking a peaceful and democratic transition to a post-apartheid society. In 1990, after 27 years of imprisonment, Mandela was released from prison, a testament to his indomitable spirit and the power of recalibration in the face of adversity.

Upon his release, Mandela continued his lifelong mission to dismantle apartheid and establish a democratic

FOURTEEN

South Africa. He and the ANC engaged in negotiations with the government, leading to the first democratic elections in South Africa's history in 1994. In a remarkable turn of events, Mandela was elected as the country's first black president, marking the beginning of a new era of hope and reconciliation for the nation.

As president, Mandela faced the daunting task of healing a deeply divided country, still grappling with the scars of apartheid. His ability to recalibrate his perspective and embrace a spirit of forgiveness and unity was instrumental in guiding South Africa through this challenging period. Mandela established the Truth and Reconciliation Commission, which provided a platform for victims and perpetrators of apartheid-era crimes to confront their past and seek forgiveness, fostering a sense of healing and unity.

Nelson Mandela's presidency marked a period of significant progress for South Africa, as the country moved towards greater equality and democracy. His leadership and unwavering commitment to justice inspired millions and left a lasting impact on the nation and the world.

After completing his term as president, Mandela continued his work as an advocate for peace, justice, and human rights, both in South Africa and globally. He established the Nelson Mandela Foundation, which focuses on promoting freedom and equality, and the Mandela-Rhodes Foundation, which offers scholarships to young Africans for postgraduate study.

His journey from prisoner to president demonstrates that even the most daunting challenges can be overcome with determination, courage, and an unwavering belief in one's ability to create change. His legacy continues to inspire and motivate individuals around the world to fight for justice, equality, and freedom.

FIFTEEN
SOARING TO NEW HEIGHTS - THE STORY OF NKOSI JOHNSON

Nkosi Johnson was born on February 4, 1989, in Johannesburg, South Africa. His early years were marked by immense challenges, as he was born with HIV during a time when the AIDS epidemic was ravaging the country. Nkosi's life would become a powerful symbol of resilience and recalibration, as he used his circumstances to raise awareness about HIV/AIDS and fight for the rights of those affected by the disease.

Nkosi's biological mother, Nonthlanthla Daphne Nkosi, was also HIV-positive. She was unable to care for her son due to her deteriorating health and the social stigma surrounding the disease. At just two years old, Nkosi was taken in by a compassionate woman named Gail Johnson, who ran a care center for children with HIV/AIDS.

Under Gail's care, Nkosi grew up in a loving and supportive environment, but he faced numerous health challenges due to his condition. Despite his illness, Nkosi showed incredible resilience and an indomitable spirit, embracing life and refusing to let his circumstances define him.

As Nkosi grew older, he began to experience firsthand the discrimination faced by those living with HIV/AIDS. He was initially denied admission to a local primary school due to his status, but with Gail's support, he fought for his right to attend. This marked the beginning of Nkosi's journey as an advocate for HIV/AIDS awareness and the rights of those affected by the disease.

Nkosi's determination and ability to recalibrate his life in the face of adversity soon caught the attention of the media. He began speaking publicly about his experiences, raising awareness about HIV/AIDS and the challenges faced by those living with the disease. His courage and eloquence captivated audiences and made him a powerful spokesperson for the cause.

In 2000, at just 11 years old, Nkosi was invited to speak at the 13th International AIDS Conference in Durban, South Africa. There, he delivered a powerful speech, calling on the South African government and the international community to do more to combat the AIDS epidemic and support those affected by the disease. His words resonated with millions, drawing global attention to the plight of those living with HIV/AIDS and the urgent need for action.

Nkosi's speech at the conference marked a turning point in his life, as he became a symbol of hope and resilience for millions of people affected by HIV/AIDS worldwide. He

FIFTEEN

continued to use his platform to advocate for the rights of those living with the disease, calling for greater access to antiretroviral treatment and an end to the stigma surrounding HIV/AIDS.

In addition to his advocacy work, Nkosi and Gail cofounded Nkosi's Haven, a nonprofit organization providing shelter, care, and support for HIV-positive mothers and their children in Johannesburg. Through Nkosi's Haven, countless families have been given a chance at a better life, free from discrimination and with access to the care and support they need.

Despite his deteriorating health, Nkosi continued to raise awareness and fight for the rights of those affected by HIV/AIDS until his death on June 1, 2001, at the age of 12. His life may have been tragically short, but his impact was immense. Nkosi's courage and resilience in the face of adversity inspired a nation and the world, bringing much-needed attention to the AIDS epidemic and the challenges faced by those living with the disease.

Nkosi's legacy continues to inspire people around the world today. His story serves as a powerful reminder of the power of recalibration and resilience in the face of adversity. Nkosi's unwavering determination to make a difference in the lives of those affected by HIV/AIDS demonstrates that even the most difficult circumstances can be overcome with courage, compassion, and an unshakable belief in one's ability to create change.

In a world where many people face adversity and struggle, Nkosi Johnson's story offers hope and inspiration.

By sharing his journey, he encourages others to recalibrate their own perspectives, to view their challenges not as insurmountable obstacles but as opportunities for growth and self-discovery.

SIXTEEN
THE UNWAVERING RESILIENCE - THE STORY OF CHRIS GARDNER

Chris Gardner was born on February 9, 1954, in Milwaukee, Wisconsin. His early years were marked by poverty, domestic violence, and a tumultuous family life. Despite these challenges, Gardner's story would become one of incredible recalibration, resilience, and triumph over adversity.

As a child, Chris and his siblings faced numerous struggles, including periods of homelessness, as they moved from one foster home to another. His mother, Bettye Jean, was a strong and determined woman who worked tirelessly to provide for her children. She instilled in Chris the importance of self-reliance, education, and hard work, lessons that would guide him throughout his life.

After a brief stint in the U.S. Navy, Chris moved to San Francisco in the late 1970s, where he began working as a medical equipment salesman. It was during this time that he met and married Sherry Dyson, but the marriage soon ended in divorce. Chris then met Jackie Medina, with whom he had a son, Christopher Jarrett Gardner Jr. As a father, Chris was determined to provide a better life for his son than he had experienced in his own childhood.

In the early 1980s, Chris experienced a life-changing encounter with a well-dressed man driving a red Ferrari. When Chris asked the man what he did for a living, he learned that the man was a stockbroker. This chance encounter sparked a new ambition in Chris, who realized that a career in finance could be his ticket out of poverty.

Determined to change his life, Chris began knocking on doors of brokerage firms, seeking an opportunity to break into the world of finance. He eventually landed an interview with Dean Witter Reynolds, a prominent investment firm. Chris was accepted into the firm's training program, but the position was unpaid, forcing him to recalibrate his expectations and find creative ways to support his family while pursuing his new career.

Chris and his young son faced immense challenges during this period, including periods of homelessness and hunger. Despite these hardships, Chris remained committed to his goal, showing up to work every day in a suit and tie, determined to succeed in his new career. His unwavering determination and ability to recalibrate his perspective in the face of adversity allowed him to persevere through these difficult times.

After completing the training program, Chris was hired as a full-time stockbroker at Dean Witter Reynolds. His hard work and determination paid off, and he quickly began

SIXTEEN

earning a significant income. In 1987, Chris founded his own brokerage firm, Gardner Rich & Co., in Chicago, a testament to his ability to recalibrate his life and achieve success despite the most challenging circumstances.

Chris Gardner's story gained widespread attention in 2006 with the release of his autobiography, "The Pursuit of Happyness," which chronicled his journey from homelessness to becoming a successful entrepreneur. The book was later adapted into a critically acclaimed film starring Will Smith as Chris and Jaden Smith as his young son.

In addition to his success in the world of finance, Chris has become a motivational speaker, sharing his story and inspiring others to recalibrate their own lives and overcome adversity. His message of resilience and determination has resonated with audiences around the world, demonstrating the power of the human spirit to triumph over even the most difficult circumstances.

As a philanthropist, Chris has used his success to give back to his community and help others facing challenges similar to those he once faced. He has supported numerous charitable organizations, including the Glide Memorial United Methodist Church in San Francisco, which provided shelter and support to Chris and his son during their time of homelessness.

Today, Chris Gardner's story serves as a powerful reminder of the power of recalibration, resilience, and the human spirit. His journey from a childhood marked by poverty and instability to becoming a successful entrepreneur and philanthropist demonstrates that even the most daunting challenges can be overcome with hard work, determination, and an unwavering belief in oneself.

Chris Gardner's journey is a great example of the transformative power of recalibration. By reassessing his goals and the path to achieving them, he was able to break free from the cycle of poverty and build a successful career and a better life for his family. His story teaches us that no matter what circumstances we find ourselves in, we have the power to change our trajectory and achieve greatness.

SEVENTEEN
TEMPLE GRANDIN - OVERCOMING CHALLENGES TO BECOME AN EXPERT IN ANIMAL BEHAVIOR

Temple Grandin's journey to success is a remarkable one that is rooted in her passion for animals, her determination to overcome the challenges of autism, and her unwavering commitment to making a difference in the world.

Born in Boston in 1947, Grandin was diagnosed with autism at a young age. As a child, she struggled to communicate with others and was often misunderstood by those around her. However, she found solace in animals and developed a deep connection with them that would shape her career.

Growing up, Grandin's family owned a ranch in Arizona, where she spent much of her time. She observed the behavior of the animals on the ranch and began to develop an understanding of their needs and habits. This early interest in animal behavior would eventually lead her to pursue a career in the field.

Despite facing significant challenges in her early life, Grandin was determined to succeed. She attended school at a time when very little was known about autism, and she struggled to fit in with her peers. However, with the support of her family and a few key mentors, she was able to develop her skills and find her place in the world.

Grandin's interest in animal behavior led her to pursue a degree in psychology at Franklin Pierce College. She went on to earn a master's degree in animal science from Arizona State University and a Ph.D. in animal science from the University of Illinois.

Along the way, Grandin faced many challenges related to her autism. She struggled with sensory overload, which made it difficult for her to function in certain environments. However, she found ways to cope with these challenges, such as by wearing earplugs and sunglasses to reduce sensory input.

Despite these challenges, Grandin continued to pursue her passion for animal behavior. She became an expert in the field of livestock handling and welfare, and she is credited with developing more humane methods of handling animals in slaughterhouses and other settings.

Grandin's work in the field of animal behavior has had a significant impact on the industry. Her designs for livestock handling facilities and equipment have been widely adopted, and her influence on animal welfare has been recognized by organizations around the world.

In addition to her work in animal behavior, Grandin has become an advocate for autism awareness. She has used her platform to raise awareness about the condition and to promote understanding and acceptance of people with autism. Her story has inspired countless people with autism, and she is widely regarded as a role model and source of hope for the autism community.

Grandin has also become a successful author and public speaker. She has written numerous books on the subject of animal behavior and autism, and she has given countless talks and presentations on these topics. Her work as a public speaker has been particularly impactful, as she has been able to share her personal story and inspire others with her message of hope and resilience.

Throughout her life, Grandin has faced many challenges related to her autism. However, she has refused to let these challenges define her. Instead, she has focused on her passions and on making a difference in the world. Her story is a testament to the power of perseverance and resilience, and serves as an inspiration to us all.

As we reflect on Grandin's journey, we are reminded of the importance of pursuing our passions and of never giving up in the face of adversity. Grandin's story is a reminder that anything is possible when we are committed to our goals and willing to work hard to achieve them. Her legacy serves as a powerful reminder that even the most difficult challenges can be overcome with determination and resilience.

EIGHTEEN
THE UNBREAKABLE SPIRIT - THE STORY OF NICK VUJICIC

Born on December 4, 1982, in Melbourne, Australia, Nick Vujicic entered the world with a rare congenital condition called tetra-amelia syndrome. This condition left him without arms and legs, a fact that shocked and devastated his loving parents. As they faced an uncertain future, they could not have predicted the extraordinary life their son would eventually lead.

Throughout his childhood, Nick faced innumerable challenges, both physical and emotional. He struggled to fit in with other children, who often stared, whispered, or excluded him from their activities. He grappled with feelings of loneliness, depression, and a lack of self-worth, which compounded his physical limitations. Life seemed bleak, and Nick even contemplated suicide at a young age.

Despite these tremendous struggles, Nick's family remained a pillar of strength, love, and support. They encouraged him to participate in everyday activities, instilling in him the belief that he was no less capable than anyone else. This steadfast encouragement and his deep-rooted faith provided the foundation upon which Nick began to rebuild his life.

As Nick recalibrated his perspective and adapted to his circumstances, he developed innovative methods to overcome his physical limitations. He taught himself to write using his mouth, type with his toes, and even swim using his torso. As he honed these skills, his confidence soared, and he realized that his life had a greater purpose: to inspire others and help them overcome their own adversity.

Nick began speaking to small groups, sharing his story and the lessons he had learned about resilience, hope, and the power of recalibration. As word of his incredible spirit spread, Nick found himself traveling the world as an inspirational speaker, touching the lives of millions with his message.

In 2005, Nick founded Life Without Limbs, a nonprofit organization dedicated to spreading his message of faith, hope, and resilience worldwide. Through this organization, Nick has reached millions of people, empowering them to recalibrate their perspectives on life and embrace their challenges as opportunities for growth.

Nick's impact on the lives of others has been profound, and he has been recognized with numerous awards and honors for his work. However, his influence extends beyond the lecture halls and stages where he speaks. His story has been featured in numerous media outlets, including television shows, newspapers, and magazines, allowing his message to reach an even wider audience.

EIGHTEEN

In 2012, Nick published a bestselling book called "Life Without Limits," which details his journey and offers practical advice for overcoming obstacles. The book quickly became an international bestseller, further expanding the reach of his message.

Throughout his life, Nick has embraced his challenges as opportunities for personal growth and transformation. He has defied the odds by marrying the love of his life, Kanae, and becoming a father to four beautiful children. He continues to travel the world, sharing his story and inspiring others to believe in their potential, no matter the obstacles they face.

As Nick's story demonstrates, the power of recalibration is immense. By adjusting our perspective and embracing adversity, we can find the strength to overcome our challenges and achieve greatness. Nick's unbreakable spirit and resilience serve as a reminder that no matter what obstacles we face, it is possible to recalibrate our lives and turn our struggles into opportunities for growth.

In today's world, where so many people face adversity and hardships, Nick Vujicic's story offers a beacon of hope and inspiration. His life is a testament to the power of the human spirit and the resilience that lies within each of us. By sharing his journey, Nick encourages us all to recalibrate our own perspectives, to see our challenges not as insurmountable obstacles, but as opportunities for growth and achievement.

Nick's journey has not been without its difficulties, but through perseverance and determination, he has managed to turn what many would consider a life of limitations into one of incredible accomplishments. His passion for helping others has driven him to continue pushing boundaries, proving that the only limits we truly have are the ones we place on ourselves.

The story of Nick Vujicic is not just about overcoming physical limitations; it is about the power of the human spirit to transcend adversity in all its forms. It is about recognizing that we are more than our circumstances, and that by recalibrating our mindset, we can unlock our true potential.

Today, Nick continues to inspire millions of people around the world through his speaking engagements, books, and social media presence. His unwavering commitment to helping others recalibrate their lives serves as a constant reminder that we are all capable of overcoming the obstacles we face.

Nick Vujicic's story is a shining example of the power of recalibration in action. By embracing adversity and using it to his advantage, he has been able to achieve remarkable things in his life and inspire countless others to do the same.

His journey serves as an inspiring reminder that no matter the adversity we face, it is possible to overcome it and achieve greatness in life. By recalibrating our perspectives, we can harness the strength within ourselves and turn our struggles into the fuel that drives us toward a brighter, more fulfilling future.

NINETEEN
THE LONG ROAD TO FAME - THE STORY OF VIOLA DAVIS

As I read Viola Davis's story, I was struck by how her journey to success was far from easy. Born into poverty in St. Matthews, South Carolina, Davis faced numerous challenges throughout her childhood. She often went hungry, and her father struggled with alcoholism. Despite these obstacles, Davis showed an early interest in acting and participated in local theater productions, demonstrating her talent and passion from a young age.

Born in 1965 in St. Matthews, South Carolina, Viola Davis grew up in a family of six children, often going hungry as a child. Her father was a horse trainer who struggled with alcoholism, adding to the family's difficulties. Despite the challenges she faced, Davis demonstrated an early interest in acting, participating in local theater productions throughout her childhood.

After graduating from high school, Davis attended Rhode Island College, initially studying to become a teacher. However, she eventually switched to theater and earned a Bachelor of Fine Arts degree from the institution. She then attended the prestigious Juilliard School in New York City, where she studied under the tutelage of renowned acting coach Lloyd Richards.

Despite her talent and training, Davis found it difficult to land roles in Hollywood due to the lack of diversity and opportunities for Black actresses at the time. She often found herself playing minor roles or struggling to find work altogether. In an interview with The New York Times, Davis shared that she once went on a string of 22 auditions without landing a single role.

This discrimination and lack of opportunities took a toll on Davis's mental health. She struggled with self-doubt and imposter syndrome, even after achieving great success in her career. In an interview with Forbes, she shared that even after winning her Academy Award, she still felt like she was "just a little girl from Central Falls, Rhode Island, who's getting lucky." However, Davis's vulnerability and honesty have made her a relatable and inspiring figure to many.

Despite these setbacks, Davis persevered and continued to pursue her dream of becoming an actress. Her big break finally came in 2008 when she was cast in the film "Doubt" alongside Meryl Streep and Philip Seymour Hoffman. Her performance in the film earned her critical acclaim and her first Academy Award nomination, finally giving her the recognition, she deserved.

NINETEEN

Davis continued to receive recognition for her performances in films such as "The Help," "Prisoners," and "Fences," the latter of which earned her the Academy Award for Best Supporting Actress. Beyond her film work, Davis found success in television, starring in the hit show "How to Get Away with Murder" for six seasons and earning critical praise and numerous award nominations for her performance.

Throughout her career, Davis has been an advocate for greater diversity in Hollywood and has spoken out about the challenges faced by Black actresses. She has used her platform to champion the work of other Black artists and to push for greater representation in the industry. In her acceptance speech at the 2015 Emmy Awards, Davis spoke about the importance of representation, saying, "The only thing that separates women of color from anyone else is opportunity."

Davis's honesty and advocacy have had a significant impact on the entertainment industry, and she continues to be a force for change. In a 2018 interview with Variety, she spoke candidly about the challenges she faced, saying, "I have a career that's probably comparable to Meryl Streep, Julianne Moore, Sigourney Weaver. They all came out of Yale, they came out of Juilliard, they came out of New York University. They had the same path as me, and yet I am nowhere near them. Not as far as money, not as far as job opportunities, nowhere close to it."

Davis's advocacy extends beyond Hollywood, as she is also an advocate for various causes, including childhood hunger, women's health, and equal pay. She has used her platform to raise awareness about these issues and to push for change, demonstrating her commitment to using her influence for positive change.

Davis's journey to success is a testament to the power of perseverance and dedication. Despite facing numerous obstacles throughout her life, she never gave up on her dreams of becoming an actress. Her talent and hard work have brought her to the heights of success, and her journey serves as an inspiration to all those who face their own winding roads to success.

Through her work and advocacy, Davis has become a trailblazer and an inspiration to many. She has shattered barriers and paved the way for other Black actresses to follow in her footsteps. Her story is a reminder that there is no single path to achieving one's goals, and that success often requires resilience and determination.

As I read Viola Davis's story, I am struck by how she has used her platform to advocate for greater representation and change. Her advocacy for issues such as diversity and childhood hunger demonstrate her commitment to using her influence to create a better world. Her story serves as a source of inspiration to those navigating their own winding roads to success and as a reminder of the importance of using one's influence for positive change.

Her story is a source of inspiration for anyone facing obstacles on their own journey, demonstrating that with hard work, perseverance, and a commitment to change, anything is possible. Her honesty and advocacy have had a significant impact on the entertainment industry, and she continues to be a force for change both on and off-screen.

NINETEEN

In the words of Viola Davis, "The only thing that separates women of color from anyone else is opportunity." Her advocacy for greater representation and change serves as a reminder of the importance of using one's voice to create a more equitable and just world, and her story serves as an inspiration to all those who aspire to make a difference.

TWENTY
A SKY FULL OF DREAMS - THE STORY OF CHRIS MARTIN

Chris Martin, the lead singer and co-founder of the globally renowned band Coldplay, was born on March 2, 1977, in Exeter, England. His journey to becoming one of the most successful and influential musicians in history was filled with adversity, but through resilience, recalibration, and determination, he transformed his life and inspired millions.

Growing up, Chris developed a love for music and started playing the piano at a young age. His passion led him to attend the prestigious University College London, where he studied Ancient World Studies. It was here that he met Jonny Buckland, Guy Berryman, and Will Champion, and together, they formed the band Coldplay in 1996.

The early days of Coldplay were filled with significant challenges. Chris's parents were initially unsupportive of his pursuit of a music career, believing it was an unstable profession. Furthermore, Chris faced debilitating stage fright, making it difficult for him to perform in front of audiences. Despite these obstacles, he remained dedicated to his passion for music and continued to push forward with his bandmates.

In addition to these personal struggles, the band faced numerous rejections from record labels. They also found it challenging to make a name for themselves in the competitive music industry. However, Chris and his bandmates remained steadfast in their pursuit of success, recalibrating their approach and continually refining their sound.

Coldplay's breakthrough came with the release of their debut album, "Parachutes," in 2000. The album, featuring the hit single "Yellow," received widespread acclaim and launched the band to international stardom. Over the next two decades, Coldplay would go on to release multiple successful albums, sell over 100 million records worldwide, and win numerous awards, solidifying their place in music history.

Throughout his journey, Chris Martin exemplified the power of recalibration and resilience. He embraced his stage fright and used it to fuel his performances, transforming his vulnerability into a strength. He also learned to navigate the complexities of the music industry, adapting and evolving his approach to create lasting success.

In addition to his musical accomplishments, Chris Martin has also been an advocate for numerous causes. He has worked closely with organizations like Oxfam, Make Trade Fair, and Amnesty International, using his influence to raise awareness and funds for various global issues. His dedication

TWENTY

to making a positive impact on the world further illustrates his commitment to using his success for the greater good.

Chris Martin's journey serves as a powerful reminder of the power of recalibration and resilience in the face of adversity. His story demonstrates that even the most seemingly insurmountable challenges can be overcome with determination, courage, and an unwavering belief in one's ability to create change.

ABOUT THE AUTHOR

Jeremy Bloom is a highly accomplished individual with a successful career in both athletics and business.

He is a three-time World Champion in skiing, two time Olympian, and holder of a record six straight World Cup victories in a single season. In football, he was an All-American at the University of Colorado and played professional football for the Philadelphia Eagles and the Pittsburgh Steelers.

In addition to his athletic achievements, Jeremy is also the CEO of Integrate, an enterprise SaaS company that has been used by some of the largest tech companies in the world. Under his leadership, Integrate was named "Best New Company" at the American Business Awards in New York City, and Jeremy was named by Forbes as one of the 30 under 30 executives making waves in the tech industry. He was also a finalist for the Ernst & Young Entrepreneur of the Year award. Integrate was acquired by Audax Private Equity in December 2021 for a large nine-figure sum.

Alongside his business ventures, Jeremy is also the founder of Wish of a Lifetime, a nonprofit organization that grants lifelong wishes to people over the age of 70. To date, the organization has granted over 3,000 wishes across the United States.

Outside of his professional pursuits, Jeremy continues to stay involved in the sports world as a commentator for college football and Olympic Sports Television Analyst for networks such as ESPN, Fox, NBC, and The Pac-12 Network.

Printed in Great Britain
by Amazon